I
REMEMBER

TIN · CUP

I

R E M E M B E R

TIN · CUP

*A Trip Back Through Time With Unpublished Stories
About The Famous Gold-Mining Town,*
TIN CUP, COLORADO

by

Eleanor Perry
Illustrated with Photographs

Telephone: (303) 233-5380

ELEANOR PERRY HARRINGTON
2844 Depew Street
Denver, CO 80214

Author: I REMEMBER TIN CUP

ISBN: 0-939101-00-9

Cover Photograph: Town hall, Tin Cup, Colorado. Copyright 1984 by Tom Williamson. Photograph courtesy of Tom Williamson.

⌣ ⌣

First Edition
    3   4   5   6   7   8   9

⌣ ⌣

Printed in the United States of America

Contents

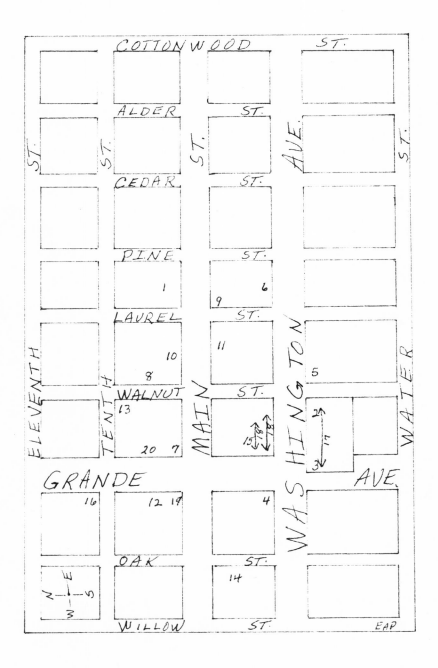

Key to Townsite Map

1. Sol Bloom's—first cabin built in Tin Cup
2. Gollagher's Store
3. Frenchy's Place
4. Town Hall
5. Aunt Kate's, Ballenger's, Hotel Rohm
6. Dr. J. McGowan's office and residence
7. Harry and Mary Morris home that burned in 1900
8. Dan and Julia Harrington home
9. W.W. Woll home
10. Samual Gollagher home
11. LaTourette home
12. Forest Service headquarters; present Tin Cup store
13. Tin Cup jail
14. Masonic Building
15. Alley buildings
16. Schoolhouse
17. Buildings destroyed in 1906 fire
18. Buildings destroyed in 1913 fire
19. Mother Lode Cafe
20. Frenchy's Cafe

For Maurice Who Believed
and
Bill and Pete Who Helped
Make It Come True

and
To the Unsung Pioneers and Early Settlers
of Tin Cup

Preface

In 1952 when I first heard stories about Tin Cup's past, I had no idea a book would result. It was not until 1972 during a trip back to Tin Cup with Frances Morris Taft and Antoinette Morris Roy, with their storehouse of memories, that I felt much of what they told me and what others later told me should be recorded. *I Remember Tin Cup* is the story of these people as they remembered happy and sad events from their childhoods, some a little vague because memories were crowded with more recent events. In some cases, newspaper items given to me gave neither the name nor the date of the newspaper. The children of those years were taught to call their elders by Mr. and Mrs.; first names could not be recalled and were added when research led me to given names. To the best of my ability, the information in this book is accurate. Due to space limitation, many stories had to be left out—perhaps there will be another book.

I Remember Tin Cup is not a history of Tin Cup, Colorado. One chapter gives the reader who is unfamiliar with Tin Cup a little background into how and why Tin Cup got its start; I've left the writing of Tin Cup's history to more capable writers. Two books covering the town's history are *History of Tin Cup, Colorado (Virginia City)* by Nolie Mumey and *Tin Cup Colorado* by Conrad F. Schader. Both books are out of print, but Mr. Schader is completing a new book on Tin Cup's history that should be available in 1987.

I regret that this book was not published before the deaths of three very special people: Maude Dobbins, Frances Taft and Antoinette Roy. They were very generous with pictures, clippings and wonderful stories. The pictures Mrs. Taft gave to me survived her home fire in 1900 and, in 1980, when my home burned, they "survived" again along with other information I had collected for this book.

Since 1952 many have contributed to the book—to all those people a special thanks. I am grateful to Becky and Tommy Williamson for getting me started again on the book. A very special thanks to Susan Gollagher Toner and Rose Gollagher Stuart for their invaluable help; to Helen Harrington and her brother, Dan Harrington, for a copy of the Louis A. Thomas article; to Dan Harrington again for filling in the gaps in the story; to Mrs. Nolie Mumey for permission to copy a picture from the late Dr. Nolie Mumey's book, *History of Tin Cup, Colorado (Virginia City)*; to my two sons, Peter and Bill, and to my sister, Marie Layson, for their patience and constructive criticism; to the Colorado Historical Society staff and especially Mercedes Penarowski and Eric L. Paddock; and to Dianne Borneman for her patience and understanding in preparing the book for publication.

Eleanor Perry
Littleton, Colorado
January 1986

A Trip Back

"It's hard to remember who lived here," said Mrs. Frances Morris Taft. "They've changed the outsides of some of these houses quite a bit." The car moved slowly down Washington Avenue's dirt road while two sisters, raised in Tin Cup, reached back 65 years to identify old log buildings—the former homes of childhood friends.

"There, that's where Mrs. Bley lived," Antoinette (Nettie) Morris Roy said. "She used to wash and iron the clothes of the dance hall girls. She must have ironed hundreds of miles of ruffles. The 'girls' had such beautiful dresses." Nettie pointed to the low, log building on the north side of Washington Avenue near the corner of Laurel Street.

"And she used to cook special dinners for the girls and their boyfriends," added Mrs. Taft. "You see, the 'girls' couldn't go to the eating places in town when they had a date. They'd make arrangements with Mrs. Bley to cook a fancy dinner and they'd eat at her house. It gave the girls a nice place to go and helped Mrs. Bley, who supported her daughter and son.

"It's beginning to come back now. This is where Gollagher's store stood." We were at the southwest corner of Washington Avenue and Walnut Street. "That's where the fire started in 1906. The shed where Mr. Gollagher kept kerosene to sell in his store was right at this corner. The fire started here and swept the whole block to Grande Avenue."

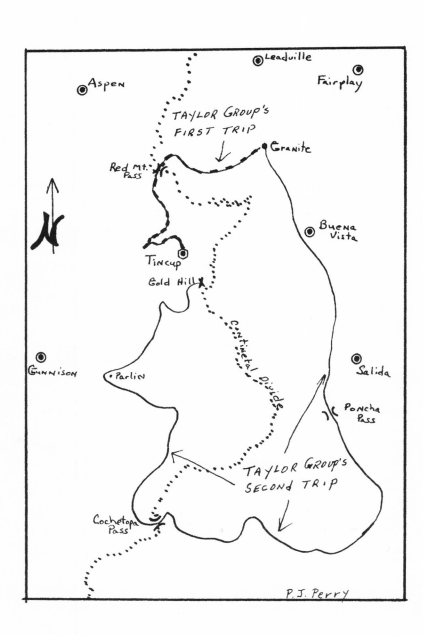

P.J. Perry

A Bit of Tin Cup History

Tin Cup, Colorado, three miles due west of the Continental Divide, was once the busiest and most productive gold-mining town in Gunnison County. It is located 47 miles northeast of Gunnison via Almont and the Taylor River road; 35 miles north of U.S. 50 via Parlin and Cumberland Pass; and 33 miles southwest of Buena Vista via Cottonwood Pass and Taylor Park. All three routes are easily accessible by car; by September 1986, the Taylor River road will be blacktopped all the way to Taylor Park.

The first known gold prospectors into Tin Cup were Jim Taylor, Gus Lamb, and Ben and Charlie Gray. In the early fall of 1859 following a summer of prospecting in Leadville, they set up their winter camp eighteen miles south of Leadville near Granite, Colorado. Shortly after the men settled into camp, a band of Ute Indians passed through Granite headed west. Jim Taylor, eager to find a trail over the Continental Divide, followed the Indians until he reached the summit of Red Mountain Pass, where he saw below a large river winding its way through a park where a herd of buffalo grazed on native grass.

Returning to camp, Taylor told his three companions about this spectacular sight just over the mountain range. It was getting too late in the year to be exploring unknown mountain territory, but the men decided to take a look at this park and try their hand at prospecting in the tributaries of the river.

It was not an easy trip over the Divide and "just over the mountain" turned out to be six miles down an arduous trail;

however, the next night found the men camped at the head of Taylor Canyon. During the night, lady luck smiled on them— their horses broke loose and wandered off. Had the men continued on down the canyon, they might never have discovered gold at all.

Their horses' tracks led the men back into the park, south of the river and up Willow Creek. A day's search and short trips into draws panning for gold found the men and their horses six miles south of the river in a forested area that was to become Tin Cup. Before making camp for the night, Ben Gray went to the nearby stream for a drink of water; the creek gravel looked promising to Gray. He scooped up some water and gravel in his tin cup and was rewarded with gold color. Thus the name "Tin Cup."

A winter storm caught the men in the high mountains. With sheer perseverance they managed to survive a mountain blizzard at Red Mountain Pass and arrived at their winter camp minus two horses but with their lives.

In March 1860, fearing they might be followed by other gold prospectors wintering at Granite, the Taylor party went back into the Tin Cup area through a long, roundabout southern route. (They were followed by Fred and Carl Siegel, Fred Lottis and Carl Niederhut.) Taylor and his group headed south to Brown's Camp (near Salida), over Poncha Pass, up Saguache Creek to Cochetopa Pass and eventually made their way to the flats west of Monarch Pass, where they found snow-free feed for their horses. After a few days of rest for themselves and their horses, the men headed west along Tomichi Creek until they reached Quartz Creek (at Parlin). Turning north, they followed the Quartz to Gold Creek (Ohio City) and then west to the head of Gold Creek, where they made camp. While the horses rested, two of the men climbed Fairview Mountain hoping to spot landmarks in the Taylor Park area. It was from this vantage point that they saw the mountain range that guided them back into the Tin Cup area.

After many backbreaking trips, the men brought their supplies and horses over the mountain to the Gold Cup area on Gold Hill. It was early April and the snow was about six feet deep! (The Siegel group headed northwest from the head of

Ben Gray's cabin in Bertha Gulch, 1953, tourists unknown. Gray wintered in a small cabin on Grande Avenue in Tin Cup.

Gold Creek into what would become Union Park.)

Taylor and his men built shelters immediately and as soon as the streams flowed in mid May, they successfully prospected for placer gold in the many streams in and around Tin Cup.

When they left in the fall, Charlie Gray, Jim Taylor and Gus Lamb left prospecting behind, headed south and joined the Confederate Army to fight in the Civil War. Ben Gray spent that winter in Denver and the following summer he went to Montana, where he struck it rich again; but his heart must have been in Colorado because he returned the next summer and built a cabin in Bertha Gulch, where he did most of his prospecting for about thirty years more. His brother, Charlie, joined him when the Civil War ended. Taylor and Lamb are lost to history.

In the late 1870s, two significant events triggered the gold rush to Tin Cup. First, Leadville, that illustrious city in the clouds, was overflowing with prospectors and miners hoping to put down a shovel and come up with riches; by the late '70s, millionaires like Horace Tabor, David Moffatt and Marshall Fields had claimed all likely looking silver or gold prospecting streams, hillsides and holes in the mountains.

Many prospectors in Leadville turned to work for wages just to survive or trekked over the Divide for golden pastures not

Sol Bloom's cabin built in 1877.

yet claimed. Sol Bloom wandered over the mountain range in 1877, saw the possibilities for a rich strike, and built the first log cabin in Tin Cup—a sturdy one-room cabin with one window and door, both facing south. The cabin stands today, has been upgraded and is a summer residence.

The next major event to trigger the gold rush happened in 1878. A Captain Hall, grubstaked by Carl Hord of Denver, found the mother lode on Gold Hill that eventually became the Gold Cup Mine. Hall returned to Denver, made no secret of his gold lode discovery and the gold rush to Tin Cup was on in earnest.

Different population figures for Tin Cup have been published, ranging from 500 to 6,000. During the gold boom, it is possible there were as many as 5,000 people if you count all the prospectors in the hills, the town population and everyone in the entire Tin Cup mining district from the north end of Taylor Park to the south end at Cumberland Pass. The town itself never housed 5,000 to 6,000 people, which would have required several high-rise apartment buildings.

By 1879, the town was unofficially known as Tin Cup Camp and was growing rapidly. Sturdy log homes were built, businesses sprang up quickly, and some unlucky prospectors turned to business, opened up saloons, gambling halls and dance halls and raked in the gold dust. In 1880, Tin Cup Camp was incorporated under the name of Virginia City.

The U.S. Post Office Department decided there was too much confusion with the mails between Virginia City, Nevada; Virginia City, Montana and now Virginia City, Colorado, and urged the Colorado citizens to change the name of their town. The townspeople took sides, one group wanting to keep the name Virginia City and the other fighting for the name of Tin Cup.

After two years of bitter quarreling and indecision, a town meeting was called to decide upon a name. Following a long, stormy session, the name was changed and the town was re-incorporated under the name, Tin Cup.

Tin Cup, Colorado, circa 1885. *Courtesy Frances Taft.*

Frenchy's Place, 1896. Frenchy, right, holding reins; Dr. J. McGowan in front of door; Sim Irie to right of doctor; Frank Korn on horse in center foreground. *Courtesy Frances Taft.*

Horse and wagon lost at inlet of Lake Catherine when Will Niederhut had mail route. *Courtesy Johanna Niederhut.*

In 1884, Tin Cup boasted of two banks, one hardware store, a bakery, two drugstores, two meat markets, five grocery stores and two hotels. The population in town was approximately 500 but nearby mines swelled the population to about 1,500. The picture on page 9 shows how the "metropolis" of Tin Cup appeared in 1883 with the new two-story Masonic building in the right background. The false-front stores, left center, were located on the south side of Washington Avenue.

As befitting a wide open and wild mining town, saloons and gambling houses outnumbered other businesses in 1883 by a wide margin. There were 26 saloons scattered along the two main streets, but Frenchy's Place commanded the key location at the busy corner of Grande Avenue and Washington Avenue. The owner—Art Napoleon Perault.

The main link to the rest of the world was St. Elmo via 12,156-foot-high Alpine Pass (now Tin Cup Pass). Mail, food, mining supplies and passengers crossed the Continental Divide every day to connect with trains and stage coach lines at St. Elmo. The journey was not without its hazards even in the summer months; the wagon trail skirted Lake Catherine (Mirror Lake) at the very foot of the Divide.

The one-way trip from St. Elmo to Tin Cup was only 12 miles—approximately six miles from St. Elmo to Alpine Pass with passengers enjoying a gradual climb through open meadows and forests of evergreens. The western side of the pass was a different story.

This was perhaps the roughest trip in the west over a narrow wagon trail with boulders, deep ruts and a drop of about 1,200 feet to Lake Catherine in the summer months. Winter brought howling blizzards, deep snows and temperatures as low as 50 below zero. Long, long poles in the deep snow guided the sleigh and toboggan drivers along the winter trail. Passengers dressed in their warmest clothes, bundled up in heavy lap robes and prayed a lot—especially mothers.

In March 1892, Mrs. Harry Morris, accompanied by her one-year-old daughter, Frances, went to her sister's home in Aspen to await the arrival of her second child. Nettie was born in April and six weeks later Mrs. Morris, Frances and Nettie returned to Tin Cup via St. Elmo and Alpine Pass. Fresh snow

Alpine Pass. Mike Hines in back at "X." *Courtesy Johanna Niederhut.*

had fallen through the night and sure enough, what happened often on these trips happened—the sleigh tipped over in the soft snow. Everyone was tossed into the snow, and when the passengers and driver had gathered their wits, Mrs. Morris was screaming frantically, "My baby—my baby is gone!" Nettie had flown out of Mrs. Morris' arms when they were tossed from the sleigh. Everyone searched carefully in the soft snow on either side of the trail, until finally one of the passengers pulled a tiny bundle from the snow. It was Nettie still bundled up and sound asleep.

But let's get back to reminiscing—

North side of Washington Avenue, 1885. Abbie Weston by baby carriage; Dr. McGowan by young boy; notice carbide lamp on post. *Courtesy Maude Woll Dobbins.*

People of Tin Cup

The Phil Korn Family

It was the spring of 1879 when Phil Korn and his brother, Dan, left Denver on horseback headed for a summer of prospecting in Leadville. They made an overnight stop in South Park at a "rendezvous camp" near present-day Antero Junction. The camp was frequented by travelers such as the Korn brothers, gold and silver prospectors, trappers and Indians.

Sitting around a fire that evening, the two Denver men listened as others talked excitedly about gold and silver strikes. When Phil and Dan Korn said they were headed for Leadville to try their luck at prospecting, other men said, "No, no. You must go over the mountain to Tin Cup Camp. That's where the gold is." Directions to the new camp were very vague.

After the others had crawled into their blanket rolls, the Korn brothers weighed the possibilities of this new gold camp against Leadville and after much serious deliberation decided to try their luck at Tin Cup Camp. At dawn they prevailed upon a half-breed staying at the camp, Johnny Roubideaux, to guide them over the mountains to the new camp.

Roubideaux led the men west from the rendezvous camp along the wagon trail until they reached the Arkansas River. Crossing the river, they turned south, followed the Arkansas to Chalk Creek (Nathrop) and then west again until they reached the Forest City settlement (St. Elmo). From here the three men climbed the old Indian trail over Alpine Pass (Tin Cup Pass today) and dropped down into Tin Cup Camp.

"They arrived late in the day and set up camp on the edge of the settlement," said Dan Harrington, grandson of Phil. "But before settling in for the night, they knew they had made a mistake. It was a wide open town with carousing and drunken brawls going on continuously, but worse yet, some of the miners used their pistols freely and stray bullets came close to where the two men were going to bed down. They quickly broke camp and moved west across West Willow Creek to the foot of Rothschild Mountain, where it was quieter and safer."

Sol Bloom had built his cabin in 1877, but few others had been built by 1879. Tents were a common sight but lacking tents, men just rolled out their blankets and slept on the ground. A "saloon" was a barrel of whiskey and a plank across two tree stumps. Summer saw the quick construction of wooden business buildings, homes and hotels to accommodate the overwhelming influx of prospectors; a town was developing and the town needed a name.

"My grandfather and great-uncle, Dan, had a hand in naming the town, Virginia City, that summer," Dan continued. "Decisions such as naming a town, plotting a townsite and assigning lots were made at the rough log bar of a saloon. The official naming of the town, Virginia City, however, was made in a log cabin constructed that summer on the west side of Grande Avenue near the bridge."

Before they were "snowed in," Phil and Dan Korn left the camp via Red Mountain Trail (Lake Creek Pass today) and Leadville and returned to Denver, where Phil Korn had a successful bootery he had left in the hands of trusted employees.

"My grandfather's boot shop was on 16th Street where the downtown Joslins store stands today," Dan said. "He, my grandmother, Marie, and my mother, Julia, born in 1879, lived in a large log home on Stout Street where the United States Post Office stands today."

Phil and Dan returned to prospecting through the summer of 1880 and divided their time between Virginia City and Leadville. In 1881, Phil sold his Denver business and moved his family that now included a son, Frank, to Virginia City, where he opened a boot shop in a building set back off Grande Avenue.

According to the Louis A. Thomas article in the *Gunnison News Champion*, July 13, 1950, courtesy Dan Harrington and his sister, Helen Harrington:

> John Philip Korn was also a cobler. He made miner's boots, cowboy boots and ladies shoes. The shoes he made were strong and tough. One of the tragedies of my young life was the loss of a pair of these shoes (almost new) that I took off and set out to dry after wading in the ditch. John Weston's pup carried them away and chewed them up. Korn made boots for Frenchie but could never make the heels high enough to compensate for his shortness in stature.

Phil Korn prospected as time allowed but for the most part his livelihood came from making shoes, saddles, harnesses and boots until his death in Salida in 1916.

In a house built in 1893, Marie Korn and her son, Frank, lived in Tin Cup year round until 1918 when they took up winter residence in Salida, returning each summer to their home in Tin Cup. "I believe I am safe in saying that my Grandmother Korn and my uncle, Frank, were the last pioneers in Tin Cup," Dan said. "They left Tin Cup for the last time in the fall of 1932 for their Salida home. During the winter, they both developed pneumonia and died within two days of each other. They are buried in Buena Vista."

Dan Korn summered in what became Tin Cup but spent the better part of his life in Leadville and Denver. He died at the age of 102.

The Dan Harrington Family

"When my father, Dan Harrington, came over from Ireland, he joined an uncle in the construction business in Kansas City, Missouri, and then took up mining in Deadwood, South

Dakota, and later in Cripple Creek, Colorado. Arriving in Tin Cup in the 1890s, he became a foreman and superintendent at Forest Hill, Dorchester and most of the Tin Cup mines," said Dan Harrington.

"He and my mother, Julia, married in about 1898 and settled in Tin Cup on Walnut Street in what later became known as the Mathews' house. They had the only bathtub in town. It was a large zinc tub in a small room behind the kitchen range. (The house has been moved in recent years to the junction of the Mirror Lake Road and Washington Avenue.)

"My folks had seven children: Marie, James, Johnny (his twin died at birth and is buried on the Catholic Knoll in Tin Cup), myself and Helen, all brought into this world by Dr. McGowan; Charles Eugene was born in Gunnison.

"The Tin Cup people lived pretty much like everyone else," continued Dan. "Except that we had mail service everyday. We had a good school and enough stores to supply our needs. The winters were hard; the temperature often dropped to 30, 40 and 45 degrees below zero. Through the month of September the men spent their time getting in wood for the winter for their homes and for the school. The women ordered in barrels of food such as apples, potatoes, onions, carrots and also canned goods for the winter. We did get a little fresh produce during the winter months but there was always the danger of it freezing on the trip over the mountain.

"There were several community wells around town," Dan continued. "Kerosene and carbide lanterns (forerunner of the Coleman gas lanterns) gave light in the town hall and in the business buildings. On the main streets carbide lamps on posts were used and near the door of a business there was usually a kerosene lantern or two for extra light. Kerosene lamps were used in the homes.

"My father was superintendent at the Blistered Horn when it closed in 1918. We moved to Buena Vista and my father worked at the Mary Murphy Mine at St. Elmo through World War I. When the war ended we moved to Leadville, where Mother met Mrs. Tabor (Baby Doe). Mrs. Tabor often stopped to visit and have tea and cake with my mother when she walked from her Matchless Mine to downtown Leadville. In 1928 my folks moved to California."

Kate Fisher

Kate Fisher, a former slave and better known as "Aunt Kate," had two boarding houses in Tin Cup. Her first, possibly in 1880, was a small log building near the corner of Grande Avenue and Main Street. Her cooking fame spread in town and to the many mines nearby and her business grew so much it was necessary to find larger quarters. A larger building finally became available on the south side of Washington Avenue near Laurel Street where "Aunt Kate" opened her new rooming and boarding house, known simply as "Aunt Kate's" until the day she died.

Kate Fisher was married to another slave when they both lived in Virginia, but they were separated when sold to different slave owners. When she was freed by her master, a Mr. Fisher, she made her way west. She lived in Leadville for some time, where she operated a successful boarding house. From there she went south to Buena Vista, where she stopped briefly, and then on to Tin Cup, remaining there until her death from cancer in 1902 at 70 years of age. Following her death, the

Aunt Kate.
Courtesy Mrs. Nolie Mumey from History of Tin Cup, Colorado (Virginia City) *by Dr. Nolie Mumey.*

building was used as a hotel/boarding house by Mrs. Charles Ballenger and later still it became the Hotel Rohm.

"Aunt Kate" was dearly loved by the townspeople and the miners. The latter made her boarding house their home when they came in from the mines on payday. Bright geraniums in her front windows were a welcome sight to these men who spent the week working in dark mine tunnels. "Aunt Kate" demanded proper manners at her dining table, and when she saw a miner reach for a slice of butter with his table knife, she'd say, "Dar, use the butter knife."

"Yes, we knew and loved Aunt Kate," said Mrs. Taft. "Every Sunday after Sunday School, Mama or Grandma Morris took us to visit her and we'd sit in her pretty sitting room. Many afternoons after school we children would go to her back door and she would give us a nice treat."

Nettie remembered, "When I was little, I used to play behind Aunt Kate's restaurant because I knew she'd always call me inside and give me cookies, a piece of pie or cake. One day Mama found out what I was doing. She spanked me and sent me to bed because, as she said, 'You deliberately play there for a treat.' I answered, 'But Mama, I didn't ask her to go in, she asked me in.' "

Nettie continued, "One time Aunt Kate sent Mama a big roasted 'possum and sweet potatoes for our supper. Not one of us would touch it except Mama, who was raised in the South. We children were especially chary of everything but beef and pork.

"My mother and Mrs. Woll always called on Aunt Kate when they went calling formally. I can remember them clearly in their long sweeping dresses and feathered hats walking along the boardwalk on their way to Aunt Kate's."

Dr. John F. McGowan

Dr. McGowan arrived in Virginia City in about 1881 and for 37 years served as a faithful but eccentric doctor to the Tin Cup people. He has been called anti-social, a recluse and a drunk in most of the stories I've read about Tin Cup. Perhaps they are true, perhaps not, but let's let some people who actually knew the doctor tell us about him.

Frances Taft remembered him from her earlier years: "Dr. McGowan was from Ireland, a Catholic and very religious. Every Sunday morning he'd go to pray in a grove of trees a short distance up the Lake Catherine road. We children knew where he went and we also knew he always carried candy in his pockets, so we'd follow him up the road to his trees. He'd give us hard candy or cinnamon bark and quietly ask us to leave. He loved children and was good to all of us. At times he'd march up and down the boardwalks on Washington Avenue lecturing on religious subjects to one and all. One day, while he was marching, waving his arms and 'lecturing', he got too close to the edge of the boardwalk, stepped back and fell into the open water ditch. He came up dripping wet while the nearby men and boys laughed. To save his pride he said, 'I just did that to tickle the boys.' He really was a good man."

Dan Harrington remembers him " . . . as a good doctor with a good education. He whittled crutches for patients with broken legs or hips and made his own splints—he had to make do with what he had on hand. You might say he was a true frontier doctor.

"Doc McGowan was a very proud individual to the point that he'd saw or split his own wood after dark. He didn't want people to see him doing manual labor. After all, he was a professional man. The poor fellow almost starved to death because people didn't call for a doctor until the patient was near death.

"Yes, I've heard that doc McGowan was a drunk, but I'd say during the last quarter of his life, he was a very sober man. A tragic incident in his life changed him. One dark night he was walking home when a man attacked him and tried to rob him. The doctor was carrying a gunnysack of nails. To defend himself, he swung the bag, hit the man square on the head and killed him. From that day forward, the doctor became a devoutly religious man. You might even say a religious freak. He'd stop children on the boardwalks and ask them questions from the Catholic cathecism, whether the children were

In front of Tin Cup Hotel, 1896. Dr. McGowan is second man from left, seated. From left, Tom McAuliffe, Frank Korn, seated, Dr. McGowan, Harry Morris, Nettie Morris, Frances Morris. Man with helmet may be Chadwick the assayer. From left, back row: Mrs. Small, who ran the hotel until 1899, Mrs. Morris, fourth man from right is Mike Hines, Boswell Reid, Frenchy Perault, Sim Irie, and boy sitting in front with "X" is Wilford Woll. Others in picture are unknown. *Courtesy Rhoda Wilson Delucchi.*

Catholics or not. If the child came up with the correct answer, he or she received a malted milk lozenger."

Dr. McGowan's office was a large building near the corner of Laurel Street facing Washington Avenue. His medical rooms were in the front of the building and his office walls were littered with newspaper clippings he had collected down through the years. His living quarters were in the rear.

"By 1918," continued Mr. Harrington, "there were no stores and few people left in Tin Cup. Dr. McGowan left too and took up residence in an old shack in Pitkin. Again, he had newspaper clippings all over the walls of the small cabin. Somehow, Doc McGowan set the shack on fire—perhaps a kerosene lamp tipped over—and Doc McGowan was trapped inside. He suffered severe burns all over his body and died a few days later. He is buried in the Pitkin cemetery."

The Harry R. Morris Family

"My father, Harry R. Morris, was raised in Syracuse, New York," said Frances Taft. "He attended West Point but was unable to graduate due to a lengthy illness.

"When he recovered, he attended the University of Michigan and became a civil engineer. He and several of his classmates spent a summer at the University's summer field camp at Leadville; their picture was taken while in Leadville at the Luke and Wheeler studio and it turned out a classmate of Papa's was a future governor of Colorado—Jesse J. McDonald."

We must assume that Mr. Morris met and fell in love with Mary Amaret Nevius while he was spending the summer in Leadville. The mother of Miss Nevius ran a successful boarding house in Leadville, and this may be where the two young people met. I have no record of where Harry and Mary were married but, again, we'll assume that after graduation from college he returned to Leadville and married Miss Nevius.

Frances continued, "Papa left Leadville in late August 1881 at a crucial time in Colorado history. General McKenzie and his

Harry Morris in West
Point uniform. *Courtesy
Frances Taft.*

men were driving the Ute Indians out of the hills and their
hunting grounds west into the Gunnison area and then into
Utah.

"Papa and two friends rode their horses down the Arkansas
River from Leadville with plans to cross the Divide and go on
into Virginia City, where rich gold deposits had been found.
As the men neared Buena Vista, they saw Utes trekking
westward. The Indians had turned hostile toward the white
man, so, taking no chances, Papa and the other two men
dismounted and turned their horses loose. In a grove of trees
the men dug three holes, crawled in, covered themselves with
dirt, leaves and branches, and hid there until all the Indians had
passed through the area—it took three days!

"The men were unable to find their horses when it was safe to
travel so they tramped up the rough, steep trail over

Cottonwood Pass on foot and eventually reached Virginia City.

"Papa knew Bat Masterson and Doc Holliday!" exclaimed Frances. Both Masterson and Holliday were in Leadville at the time Mr. Morris was there. Did he also rub elbows with Jesse James while the latter was prospecting/hiding out in Leadville?

"Papa was a civil and mining engineer and a surveyor and he was very active in many ways to make Tin Cup a good place to live."

By 1884, Mr. Morris was Tin Cup's Police Magistrate, Clerk and Recorder. He later served as mayor, Justice of the Peace, was on the school board and was postmaster from about 1906 to 1908 and possibly prior to 1903.

Civil Engineer Class, Leadville. 1. C.C. Baldwin, Ann Arbor, Mich.; 2. Geo. M. Robison, East Springfield, Penn.; 3. Jesse McDonald, No. Springfield, Penn.; 4. Harry Richardson, Princeton, Ill.; 5. Harry R. Morris; 6. Fred G. Bulkley, Monroe, Mich.; 7. James McDonald, No. Springfield, Penn.; 8. Frank L. Sizen, Altawa, Ill. *Courtesy Frances Taft.*

"Grandma Morris moved to Tin Cup in 1890 and lived with us. She was a nurse and was with Mother when I was born, two months prematurely. I was told I weighed only 2½ pounds and was too tiny even for diapers," Frances reflected. "Grandma constantly warmed blankets on the reservoir of our wood-burning kitchen range to wrap me in until I had gained enough weight to be past the danger stage. Grandma helped nurse many of the children and adults while she lived in Tin Cup and helped bring many of those children into the world."

Elizabeth Van Ness Morris (Grandma Morris) was well thought of not only in Tin Cup but in Buena Vista as well, where she lived with her son, Harry, and family, from 1908 until her death in 1910. She was known as Grandma Morris by nearly everyone in Chaffee and Gunnison counties.

"Papa had a big garden every year and had good luck with leaf lettuce, radishes, rutabagas, carrots and turnips. We had so many turnips, we called our dog 'Turnip.' Our vegetables were stored for the winter months in sand in our cellar under the house. We had chickens as did many people in Tin Cup; someone gave me a rabbit, and some people kept cows. There were dogs and many cats to help keep down the field mice population. In the summer months, Mama took us raspberry picking up near Lake Catherine, along the Gold Cup Mine road and near the cemetery for raspberry pies and jam.

"The post office was in our home," said Frances. "That meant Papa had to have a large amount of money on hand at all times and people knew it. One time, Papa had to go out of town on mining business for a week, and the night he left, it turned bitter cold. Mama brought her setting hen into the kitchen and placed her near the kitchen range. During the night, someone tried to break into the house, but they made the mistake of trying to pry open the kitchen window near the stove. That set up a chain reaction.

"The hen started cackling and the cackling awakened Grandma, who slept in the bedroom off the kitchen. With the noise of the cackling hen and Grandma lighting lamps all over the house, we three children woke up and went downstairs to see what was happening. The burglar had left in a hurry, but Mama was still sleeping. She hadn't heard a thing—Mama was slightly deaf."

Nettie remembered Ben Gray. "He had a Van Dyke beard, both his hair and his beard were gray. Every month he received a money order for about $100 and cashed it at Papa's post office. The money order came from a bank and no doubt was money Mr. Gray had invested. He was still living in his cabin in Bertha Gulch and prospecting when we knew him."

The Will W. Woll Family

On September 24, 1972, Frances Taft, Nettie Roy and I spent a pleasant evening visiting with Maude Woll Dobbins in her Buena Vista home, where she told us a little about her family:

"My Dad arrived in Tin Cup in 1881. He left Denver on horseback and arrived in the busy, frontier town of Buena Vista on August 22. He stayed only one night in Buena Vista because his heart was set on prospecting for gold in Taylor Park. By horseback, he and two friends took the wagon trail over Cottonwood Pass and then north to Forest Hill. Dad's prospecting hopes were dashed at Forest Hill so he headed south to Virginia City. Again he was not lucky in finding gold in the ground, but shortly after arriving in Virginia City, Dad and Mother met and were married.

"In partnership with my grandfather, John Weston, he opened a small general supply and grocery store. A short time later Grandpa Weston went to St. Elmo and operated a store there for about two years. Upon his return to what was then Tin Cup, he acquired the Pacific Hotel and operated that for many years.

"In the meantime, Dad's business was growing. In 1904, Will Niederhut, who had a wagon and carriage repair business in Tin Cup, went into partnership with my father. Shortly after this, Dad and Mr. Niederhut bought the Masonic Building, had it moved from Oak and Main on big log rollers pulled by horses to the northeast corner of Washington and Grande Avenues and attached it to their store. The upstairs hall was used as a

Masonic Hall, for town meetings and other community functions.

"In 1911, Dad sold his share of the business to Mr. Niederhut and our family moved to Buena Vista, where Dad went into partnership with Sam Calhoun in a grocery store. He later became an undersheriff of Chaffee County."

The Gollagher Family

Susan Gollagher Toner tells about her family:

"Papa (Samuel Phillips Gollagher) came over from Ireland when he was 18. He learned the store business before leaving Ireland and served a 3-year apprenticeship there. When he arrived in New York, he worked as a night clerk in a hotel and took a bookkeeping course during the day. In 1885, he heard of the gold strikes in Colorado and headed west, arriving in Tin Cup that same year. He worked as a miner at first and then Mr. Carl Freeman hired him in his big store as a clerk because Papa was so good at figures. In 1892, Mr. Freeman opened the Bank of Tin Cup and left the store business pretty much to Papa.

"Mama (Anne Clickener) was a niece of Koertenius (Charley) LaTourette. In the spring of 1893, Aunt Emma and Uncle Korty (LaTourette) were visiting relatives in Covington,Indiana, where Mama lived. She had had malaria and wasn't too well. The LaTourettes persuaded her to return to Tin Cup with them, thinking the high altitude and clear air might help her. She did and she met Papa in Freeman's store soon after she arrived. After Mama had made several trips to the store, Papa asked her for a date, and then more dates. They were married December 28, 1893.

"In 1894 or 1895, I'm not sure, Mr. Freeman sold the store to my father. (Mr. Freeman kept the building.) Homer Smith, who had clerked for Mr. Freeman, continued on with my father, and my cousin, Tommy Gollagher, came from Australia to work for Papa, and he lived with us.

"Mama and Papa had seven children born in this order: Kathryn, Rose, myself, Anne, Gertrude, Samuel and Charles.

Before my two brothers were born, we five girls went to Indiana with Mama for a visit. Mama sewed beautifully and with wool plaid (it was winter) material from our store, Mama made each of us dresses from the same pattern but of different colors. Rose remembers hers was red and either black or brown, Kathryn's was mostly blue but we can't remember the others. When we got off the train in Denver, a *Denver Post* reporter took our picture and wrote a small article about us. Unfortunately, we have no copy.

"Papa was sort of a banker for many of the miners; on paydays they deposited part of their pay with him for safe keeping. He was also handling the payroll for one of the mines when he was robbed in 1904, I think. He was working on his books in the back of the store when two masked men entered the store; a third man stayed outside by the door. One of the masked men in the store held a gun on three local men; I believe they were Mr. Keyes, Mr. Hines and Mr. Korn. They were seated around the pot-belly stove visiting when the masked men came in." (The men may have been L.H. Keyes, John or Mike Hines, Phil or Frank Korn.)

"The other masked man went right over to Papa and said, 'Put up your hands.' Papa laughed, thinking it was some of the local boys playing a joke. The man said, 'I mean what I say, put up your hands.' Papa saw the man was mad and meant business and Papa did what he said.

"The robbers got the entire payroll of $1,200, which was a lot of money in those days. The men were never caught.

"Immediately after the robbery, Papa got a strong box to keep large sums of money in, but he needed a safe place to hide it. He kept potatoes well covered in the store cellar to keep them from freezing, and it was under the potatoes that he hid the strong box. No one knew where the strong box was hidden except Papa, Mama and his two trusted clerks, Mr. Smith and cousin Tommy. It was this strong box that was recovered after the fire destroyed our store.

"We had a comfortable two-story home on Main Street about midway between Walnut and Laurel Streets (now the Coburn summer home). 'Coyote Bill' Duran, a bachelor, lived up the hill from us in the original cabin built by Mr.

Bloom. Aunt Emma and Uncle Korty lived across the street in what is now the Carroll house.

"When Papa died, my brother Charles was only six days old. Mama was still recuperating from his birth so Aunt Emma, Grandma Morris and many other wonderful women in Tin Cup helped out while Papa was so sick. Dr. McGowan was his doctor and did all he could. We think Papa died of a heart attack.

"Homer Smith and cousin Tommy ran the store while Papa was sick, after his death and until the fire on August 15. Everyone who had money in safe keeping with Papa got their money and Bill Murdie, who 'deposited' part of his mine wages with Papa, said later, 'I got every cent owed me.' However, a few people who had charge accounts at the store never paid up.

"We left Tin Cup in October 1906 and moved to Covington, Indiana, near my mother's folks. Mr. and Mrs. C.T. Judy and their daughters, Zoe and Ruth, lived in our Tin Cup house that winter.

"Mama returned to Tin Cup in 1908 for a short visit and to settle estate business, but she never expected to return for good, so she let the house and land go for taxes. She had brought out some dishes and small furniture in 1906, but because of the high cost of freight, there was quite a bit of furniture left in the house. 'Coyote Bill' got it all for about $10 in back taxes.

"Mama led a long and useful life and died at the age of 95. Homer Smith spent the rest of his life in Tin Cup mining and prospecting. Cousin Tommy worked at the Gold Cup Mine for a time and then left for his home in Australia. He married there and had nine children."

Lowry (Larry) Englebright

Lowry Englebright was a shy and very private person, but through his years in Tin Cup and Taylor Park, he built up a host of friends, many of whom he outlived. Mr. Englebright came to Colorado from Iowa and attended Colorado College at

Colorado Springs. Before and after classes each day, Lowry worked as a baggage handler at the Colorado Springs railroad depot to help pay his college expenses. He first came into Tin Cup in 1893 and wintered that year and in '94 and '95 in Sol Bloom's cabin. For years after, there was a heavy cardboard 'plaque' just inside the doorway to the cabin indicating that Lowry Englebright had wintered in the cabin in 1895 and had registered a temperture of -52 degrees. His brother, Alva, also a miner, stayed with Lowry from time to time, and their sister, Kathryn, visited them often in Tin Cup.

"He was a loner and not outgoing," said Dan Harrington. "But he was always pleasant. Once he felt comfortable with a family, he would stop by for short visits. Lowry never rode a horse or owned one, he always walked until 1949.

"We were at the Hillerton cabin one summer day in 1949 when we heard a noise similar to a plane out of control. Rushing outside to see what was wrong, we saw, coming down our lane, a bright yellow Jeep. It was Larry and he had that Jeep

Lowry Englebright by his cabin on Grande Avenue, 1954.

in low gear and wide open and that is the way he drove that Jeep from the day he learned to drive it."

Dan Harrington recalled Mr. Englebright's mining days. "Larry was an excellent mill wright and, as an underground timberman, he was hard to beat. He worked in the West Gold hill tunnels, at the Blistered Horn, Forest Hill and the Amazon tunnel. Larry worked with my father in the mines, and he and my folks, including my grandparents and Uncle Frank, remained close friends through the years."

Ann and Archy Steinbeck, Gunnison, were friends of Lowry Englebright for many years. Ann, daughter of Margaret and Raleigh Flick, Ohio City, told me about receiving a congratulatory card from Mr. Englebright on the birth of their daughter, Lois Anne, on February 27, 1954. "On the card," said Ann, "Mr Englebright had written 'Congratulations on having a little girl; the world needs more little girls.' We treasured that card and Lois Anne has it now.

"In late June 1965, about two months after his death, a memorial service for Mr. Englebright was held in the Tin Cup town hall," recalled Vivian Osborne, Pueblo, and a Tin Cup summer resident from 1932 to 1983. "The hall was beautifully decorated with flowers in containers of moss, and many of Mr. Englebright's friends were there. When the services were over and as we left the hall, each of us was given a bouquet of wildflowers to carry in our right hands. From the hall the procession made its way, walking slowly, past Mr. Englebright's former home on Grande Avenue, east along the cemetery road to the Protestant Knoll and Mr. Englebright's grave, where the marble marker had already been set. We left our bouquets at the base of the grave marker. The procession was a beautiful thing to see and to be a part of."

The Forest Service

Even the United States Forest Service figured in Tin Cup's history.

Just five weeks before his 21st birthday, William R. Kreutzer

Forest Service headquarters, present Tin Cup Store.

became the first Forest Ranger in the United States. On August 8, 1898, W.T.S. May, Superintendent of Forests, officially appointed young Kreutzer the first Forest Ranger in May's Denver office and gave Kreutzer his first assignment, "Put out those forest fires in the Plum Creek Reserve" (later part of the Pikes Peak National Forest).

Kreutzer served in other reserves before he was made Ranger-at-Large in the Gunnison Reserve in 1905, where he served for fifteen years. All reserves became known as national forests in about 1907. Kreutzer arrived in Tin Cup on

September 24, 1905, found a small cabin to rent and set up headquarters for the Taylor Park District.

"We met Mr. Kreutzer for the first time on Halloween night while we were out 'tricking,'" said Frances Taft. "He helped us climb onto the Tin Cup Hotel roof to stuff gunnysacks down the chimney. We smoked everyone out. Mr. Kreutzer had a great singing voice and he loved to sing."

On January 1, 1907, William Kreutzer was made Supervisor of the Gunnison Reserve—800,000 acres. His headquarters were now in Gunnison, but his time was spent out in the field.

By 1955, a mountain peak due east of Tin Cup on the Continental Divide was named for Mr. Kreutzer. Just south of the East Willow Creek bridge on Grande Avenue there is a forest service sign pointing to Mt. Kreutzer.

Kreutzer Peak sign on Grande Avenue.

Charles W. Taft, the sixth United States Forest Ranger, served under Kreutzer and in the summer of 1907, Taft was in charge of installing the telephone line from Pitkin to Tin Cup with the help of a Mr. Warner. Other forest rangers, Alex McDonald and Ed Vance, completed the line from Tin Cup to Dorchester. The switchboard was in a small building just below the hill at the southwest corner of Grande and Washington Avenues with only major businesses in Tin Cup and the forest ranger station connected to the line. Sadie Hines and Frances Morris Taft were the telephone operators.

By October 1907, Taft was the ranger for the Tin Cup/Taylor Park District. Frances remembers him well, ". . . a handsome young man and I was sixteen years old and just back from a summer in New York state visiting cousins. I met him at a dance in the town hall and fell in love at first sight. My father had the post office in our home at that time and I saw Charlie often when he came for his mail.

"On September 19, 1908 (how well she remembered!) some friends and Charlie and I were on our way over Cumberland Pass by the old wagon road to attend a dance in Pitkin when he asked me to be his wife. My folks moved to Buena Vista in late 1908 and Charlie and I were married at their home on January 19, 1909. We had one son, Tom, and we spent 43 happy years together."

Business buildings on south side of Washington Avenue, 1896. The 1906 fire started just beyond the ladder at far left. Mike Hines, second from right, Frenchy Perault in shirtsleeves, Nettie Morris Roy child on left on rail. *Courtesy Frances Taft.*

Major Tin Cup Fires

At one time Tin Cup was a forest of evergreens sweeping down from the nearby mountains to the streams west of town. With the advent of settlers, many trees were cut to build homes, business buildings, wagons, furniture and for firewood.

In 1891, a town water system, complete with fire hydrants, was built in Tin Cup by a Denver plumber/prospector. Due to the heavy cost of replacing frozen and broken pipes, the water system was no longer in use by 1899; the townspeople depended on community wells and the open water ditches that ran along the main streets for water.

The Tin Cup fire wagon was located in an open leanto attached to the west side of the town hall. It came equipped with ladders, hoses and leather buckets, but was of little use in the 1906 and 1913 business district fires due to the wooden construction of the buildings and in both cases the high winds. The ladders and buckets were used to save the roofs of the buildings on the north side of Washington Avenue in the 1906 fire; hoses were useless with no water system connected to the fire hydrants.

In 1900 an early morning chimney fire destroyed the Harry Morris family home. It was a large wooden two-story home, but let's let Frances Taft tell us:

"When I was 9 years old, our house located on the northeast corner of Grande Avenue and Main Street burned to the ground. I got up early that morning and as I was dressing, I smelled smoke and looked out my bedroom window. Smoke

Fire hydrant at corner
of Grande and
Washington Avenue.

Courtesy Colorado Historical Society.

was billowing out from under the eaves of our house.

"I yelled to the folks who were downstairs in the kitchen, but it was too late to save our home. We all got out safely and while Mama and Papa tried to save a few things, I held my one-year-old brother, Edward. Nettie ran to town for help. Friends and neighbors helped my folks save some furniture and pictures and a quilt I had made. We did lose a lot of heirlooms that Mama had brought to Tin Cup. (All of Mrs. Taft's pictures used in this book were saved from the fire.)

"My father's assay office was in our house and he lost his surveying instrument worth $1,000 (a tidy sum in 1900). It was a severe financial blow, but Papa's cousin, Francis Morris of New York, sent him a new one. The people of Tin Cup were very kind and helped us with clothes, bedding and other household items. After the fire, we moved into a house on Walnut Street until Papa built us a new house on Oak Street.

"Mama lost her button box in the fire and for a long time, I hunted lost buttons on the ground under everyone's clotheslines so that Mama would have a button box again."

Frances continued with information about the disastrous business district fire in 1906. "It was 11:00 at night and Mama and I were walking uptown to mail a letter at the post office which was located in the lobby of the Tin Cup Hotel; Ed Churchill was postmaster at that time. As we rounded the corner at Grande and Washington Avenues, we heard a gunshot and looking in the direction of the noise, we saw smoke near Gollagher's store. Before we knew it, fire was all over the store. Someone rushed past us to the town hall and rang the belfry bell to alert everyone.

"There was a high wind from the east that night and the fire swept through that entire block on the south side of Washington Avenue straight through to Grande Avenue. Sparks flew across the street and there was constant danger of the business places on the north side going up in flames too.

"Every able-bodied man in town and from the nearby mines worked through the night to save the buildings on the north side. Men were on the roofs with axes cutting out the flaming spots and other men lugged pails of water to cool down the roofs and buildings. Women hauled merchandise out of the

Frances Taft, left, and Antoinette Roy near pond, standing where their home once stood. Left background: old Forest Service headquarters, present Tin Cup store; right background, old miners' cabins.

buildings across the street hoping to salvage some things in case the flames reached the north side.

"Toward morning the air got quite chilly—the men were all tired and soaked to the skin, so Mike Hines passed around liquor that he had 'rescued' from his saloon, The Cabinet, before it burned to the ground. Most of the men got drunk and their wives got mad, but, at least, the men didn't get pneumonia. The next morning the women and children carried everything back into the buildings that were saved—the men were in no condition to do it!

"By the way, Mama didn't mail her letter that night."

Rose Gollagher Stuart of West Point, California, remembers the fire well:

" . . . the 1906 fire I remember vividly. It was just about a month after my father's death. It was a *very windy night* and our cousin, Tom Gollagher, who clerked in our store and lived with us, was getting ready for bed when Mr. Whittenberger fired his pistol to alert the townspeople of the fire.

"Mother went to the living room window to see what was wrong and, just a block away, she saw fire on the east side of our store. She hollered to Tom. He ran to the store and risked his life by going inside to save the account books and a box of rifle shells near the books that he knew would endanger the lives of the fire fighters if they exploded in the fire. Because of the wind and the headstart the fire had, that was all Tom could save.

"The store safe fell through to the basement. The strong box containing a large amount of money was later found under the potatoes in the cellar. The money was scorched, but it was all redeemed by the U.S. Government. Some of the people with businesses further down the street had time to save some things before the fire consumed their buildings.

"The fire started on the east side of our store where a small building housed a coal oil tank. The side of the building had been saturated with coal oil which made it burn rapidly. Pete Whittenberger, returning home late, saw someone run from the shed just as the fire started. The fire was thought to be of incendiary origin, but this could never be proven."

"Yes, I remember the 1906 fire," said Mrs. Roberta Wilson Delucci on a brief visit to Tin Cup in 1952. "My mother was running the Tin Cup Hotel and our family lived upstairs. The ringing of the town hall bell woke us up and when we discovered our block was on fire, we grabbed what clothes we could and ran for our lives out the back door of the hotel. A lady, her name I cannot recall, took my sister, Lucinda, and me to her home on south Grande Avenue.

"A short distance from the fire I turned to look back and saw Mother push the clothes she had hung on the lines to dry that night to the far end of the lines away from the burning building. That was all she could save."

The total loss for all businesses was about $25,000 with very

Morning after 1906 fire. Notice damage to roofs across street.
Courtesy Maude Dobbins.

little insurance coverage. The Samuel Gollagher estate was the
heaviest loser with an estimated $10,000 in merchandise; C.A.
Freeman owned the building. Besides owning Frenchy's Place,
A.N. Perault owned the Tin Cup Hotel, the old post office
building and another saloon—all a total loss. Mike Hines lost
his saloon, The Cabinet. Joe Chitwood operated a bakery
which was lost in the fire, and Peter Whittenberger who
discovered the fire lost his saloon. Some of the buildings across
the street suffered roof damage.

After the fire, Frenchy Perault immediately established
another saloon in a building north of the Woll-Niederhut
store. The burned out block remained devoid of buildings for
20 years.

Despite the losses and hardships caused by this fire, some
good resulted, courtesy Maude Woll Dobbins:

BIG TIME AT TIN CUP

Last Saturday evening occurred the "swellest" social event that has taken place in Tin Cup for many years. Wm. Niederhut and W.W. Woll, of the firm of Tin Cup Mdse., Co., gave a ball in honor of those who so valiantly aided in saving their store during the fire of August 15, this year. An immense crowd was present, everyone in their finest clothes; flowers were in profusion, furnished by the hosts. To have walked into the ballroom, a stranger might have imagined he were in the city.

At 12 o'clock the guests were ushered up to the Masonic Hall where a repast fit for a king awaited them. The tables were beautifully decorated with cut flowers, and seated over 50 couples. The dancers enjoyed themselves until the "wee sma' hours," and as each one went home, felt glad to have been there. All join in one accord in pronouncing the whole affair a grand success . . .

The following is a newspaper report of the May 24, 1913 fire, courtesy Frances Taft:

FIRE DESTROYS LARGE PART OF TIN CUP

Business Section Wiped Out By Flames This Week, Ten Buildings Burn, Property Loss Will Reach $20,000; Cause of Conflagration Unknown

Nearly the entire business section of Tin Cup, a mining camp in the northern part of Gunnison County, was wiped out by fire last Friday morning, about one-thirty. It is reported that over twenty thousand dollars worth of property was destroyed. About ten buildings were burned to the ground. The cause of the fire is unknown. The flames were first discovered coming from a small room adjoining the old LaTourette saloon building. There is no water system of any kind in the town, and the only water available ran in the small irrigation ditches along the street. The buildings were all constructed of wood and when the fire once gained a headway, it consumed the buildings in a few minutes.

Tin Cup about 1915. *Courtesy Frances Taft.*

The heaviest loss was sustained by W.G. Niederhut who owned a general supply store. It is stated that his loss will reach $14,000. Other buildings destroyed are the Tin Cup Mercantile Store, LaTourette Saloon building, A.N. Perault Saloon (Frenchy's) building and residence, and the Frank Beyers building.

One store, a hotel and a livery stable are the only buildings in the business part of town which remain standing.

Frenchy lived in the back of his saloon and, according to Dan Harrington who lived in Tin Cup at that time, "Frenchy was sick in bed with pneumonia when the 1913 fire broke out. Several men ran into his living quarters shouting that he had to get up and get out before the fire reached his building. Frenchy was too sick to move and Frenchy was too heavy to move—he weighed nearly 300 pounds. His friends tore the back door off its hinges, rolled Frenchy onto the door and carried him to safety across the street and into the town hall.''

Frenchy was taken to the Salida Hospital later that day over Alpine Pass. He recovered from his bout with pneumonia and after being wiped out by two major fires, Frenchy Perault retired. Frenchy never married and he set up his first saloon when Tin Cup Camp was established in 1879. He spent the last two years of his life in Buena Vista, where he died in 1915.

Two rusted safes are all that remain today, indicating the location of the businesses that burned in 1913. The fires of 1906 and 1913 and the decline in mining in the area were the death knell for Tin Cup.

Gold Cup Mine mess hall, 1954.

Entertainment in Tin Cup

Years after leaving Tin Cup, Nettie Roy was asked by a young relative, "What did the children of Tin Cup do for fun?"

Nettie replied, "We didn't have a radio or a television set but we did have long, nearby hills for skiing and sledding. We walked to Tin Cup Lake to ice skate. When there was no school, someone would fill a sleigh with hay, go from house to house to collect children and we'd go sleigh riding to Abbeyville or Hillerton or even to the ranches in Taylor Park, singing our hearts out along the way.

"Many days we played card games at Frank Korn's home. We'd play either Sluff, Hi Fi, Uker, Hearts, 7 Up, Casino, Old Maid, Whist or 500. Horses and burros were always available to ride in town and to the nearby hills.

"Frances and I had a large collection of beautiful dolls," continued Nettie. "We made clothes for them from scraps of dress material, pieces of lace or ruffles and sometimes feathers that Mama or Grandma Morris gave us. We made glamorous dresses for our dolls. Mama would have us bring our dolls from our upstairs bedroom down to the living room on cold, snowy days and Frances and I would play make believe with our dolls for hours in the warmth of the living room stove."

Frances added, "I remember going to the nearby mines for dances when we were older. Those were gala events and we looked forward to them. You see, there was no commuting to and from the mines in those days. During the week, the miners lived in bunk houses right on the mine company's property and they took their evening meals in the large mess hall. The mine

Frances Taft on burro, Florence Reid on sled. *Courtesy Frances Taft.*

owners and supervisors knew the men needed more diversion than payday trips to Tin Cup, so they held a dance occasionally followed by a smorgasboard and invited people from Tin Cup and surrounding camps. At Gold Cup Mine, the dances were held in the big mess hall. The miners put on their best clothes and the mine supervisors and cooks outdid themselves with decorations and eye-catching 'gourmet' food.''

Another type of entertainment at Gold Cup Mine from the scrapbook of Maude Woll Dobbins, 1905:

A BANQUET AND MUSICAL

On Saturday evening, Feb. 3d, the managment and employees of the Gold Cup Mine, near Tin Cup, furnished a delightful entertainment and supper for about forty invited guests. An unusually interesting and pleasing musical program, vocal and instrumental, was rendered. The supper proved to be a veritable feast, and all those who were so fortunate as to partake thereof never tire of singing the praises of Chef Fred Ewing and his assistants.

The tables were prettily decorated, and the viands daintily served under the skillful direction of Head Waiter Harry Johnson, whom the girls say, "Looked too cute for anything" in his neat and nobby suit of white.

One and all declare it the entertainment par excellence of the winter in this community, and vote the Gold Cup boys "all jolly good fellows."

Mr. and Mrs. F.G. Edwards, Mr. L. Winsheimer, Mrs. E.O. Churchill, Misses Sadie Hines, Rhoda Wilson, Maude Woll, Mattie Smith, Ione Miller, Lena Chitwood, Marie Ketcham, Lucinda Wilson, Mrs. Millstead, Messrs. H.A. Humphrey, Chas. Ward, Lee Stidd, Wm. Murdie, Harry Williams, Joe Carson and Elbert Stidd were those present from Tin Cup.

The parents of Tin Cup enjoyed the dances in the town hall and always took their children with them. "We didn't know what babysitters were in those days," said Susan Toner.

Ione Miller Jones, a school teacher in Tin Cup, wrote in 1972, "I understand Tin Cup is becoming a great tourist attraction as a 'ghost town'. When I was there in 1904-05, it was anything but that; a lively place indeed and we danced in the town hall every Saturday night from 9:00 p.m. to 4:00 a.m."

Susan Toner recalled, "My sisters and I used to cut out and

Tin Cup town hall. *Courtesy G.L. Gebhardt.*

make our own paper dolls from the colored sections of fashion magazines. For our last Christmas in Tin Cup my sister, Anne, and I each got 'boughten' skis. We were just learning to ski and when our neighbor, Mr. Duran, saw that Anne and I were having trouble with our skis going this way and that because the snow was so soft, he came out of his house, put on his big skis and made tracks for us to follow. He stayed nearby and picked us up when we fell. He was probably the first ski instructor in Colorado!"

Susan continued, "The women of Tin Cup had quilting bees, fancy work clubs and book clubs. We even had a traveling library that came to Tin Cup regularly."

Mrs. Taft recalled, "Sunday afternoons were set aside for formal 'calls'. Mama, Grandma Morris and other women of Tin Cup would go forth in their ruffled street-length dresses, lace or fur-trimmed bonnets, white kid gloves and calling card cases in hand. They'd spend about ten minutes visiting at each home, leave their card and go on to the next house."

"Dinner invitations were very formal," added Nettie. "When Aunt Nettie (Antoinette Cattna, sister of Grandma Morris) came from Washington, D.C. to visit us one summer, she thought we'd be surrounded by a tribe of Indians and rough, ignorant, white people. Of course, we weren't.

"Shortly after she arrived, mother had a formal luncheon to introduce the ladies of Tin Cup to Aunt Nettie. Mama got out her best linen, silver, china and cut glass for the occasion, and I was delegated to deliver the formal, written invitations to the ladies. Aunt Nettie could hardly believe it when, in turn, people entertained her so delightfully in their small houses and cabins. She was also surprised to find that many parents were college graduates and that there was a good school with good teachers in Tin Cup."

"Mr. and Mrs. Johnny Hines had an organ in their home and their daughter, Sadie, played the organ well," added Frances. "We went to their home many evenings, gathered round the organ and sang. Tom McAuliff lived across the road and could hear us singing. Sometimes he'd come over and kid us, saying, 'The coyotes are howling again.' That was his excuse to stay and sing along with us.

Boating on Tin Cup Lake (Lily Pond), Dr. McGowan on log between four children. There was a road around the lake. *Courtesy Frances Taft.*

"In the summer months, boating on Tin Cup Lake on Sundays was the big event of the week. There was a boat house on the north side of the lake where the boats were tied up during the week. That boat house is gone now and the lake seems much smaller."

Children haven't really changed:

With a smile, Frances continued, "One evening Mama and Papa gave a big dinner party. The tables were set with linen, china and cut glass and were loaded with turkey, roast beef, white and sweet potatoes, turnips, carrots, rolls, pickles, cakes and pies. As with most parties in Tin Cup, everyone brought their children. After we children had eaten dinner, we were sent upstairs to play. We played the usual 'hide and seek' in and out of the bedrooms, but when that grew tiresome, we decided to attack the pillows in my room. Flying feathers are noiseless!

"Apparently we were too quiet because Mama came up to check on us and discovered us in a sea of feathers. We spent the rest of the evening gathering elusive feathers and putting them back into the ticking."

The following news items are from Maude Dobbins' scrapbook (*Gunnison News Champion*, 1905):

> Mrs. W.W. Woll entertained a party of young people at flinch last Friday evening. A delicious lunch was served after the games were played, and the following were guests: Elsie Bley, Fannie Morris, Paul Bley, Maude Woll, Nettie Morris, Wilford Woll and Bertha Williams.

> (1906 or 1907): A number of the younger social set were out serenading Wednesday night, but as they did not stop at our bungalow, cannot give names of the merry party.

> The little folks are having the time of their lives this spring. Friday evening, the 6th, Edward Morris entertained them superbly at the home of his parents with a stereopticon exhibition. Saturday evening, the 14th, little Miss Abbie Woll gave a graphophone "musicale," an instrument on which she plays beautifully. Light refreshments were served at both parties and the boys and girls enjoyed themselves as only those in childhood can. They were admirably chaperoned on each occasion by Miss Reynolds. Those in attendance were Marie Harrington, Mildred Whittenberger, Victorine LaTourette, Abbie Woll, Sarah and Margaret Tomney, Harry Whittenberger.

There were also outings at distant attractions. A favorite spot was the Wanita Hot Springs spa located about 20 miles southeast of Tin Cup. At the spa, there was a large indoor swimming pool fed by the nearby hot springs. The pool was especially attractive to the young Tin Cup people who endured subzero temperatures in winter and few days hot enough for swimming in the summer months.

Early winter snows confined Tin Cup's social life to the town, but Christmas and New Year's were eagerly awaited.

At Waunita Hot Springs, July 4, 1908. Left to right, back row: Tom Johnson, Carrie Rowland, Harry Humphrey, Sadie Hines, Fannie Morris, Ella Crowley, Willie Murdie, Squier Pearse; left to right, front row: Bob Rowland, Katie Clark, Mr. Rohm. *Courtesy Christie Wyse and Frances Taft.*

On October 17, 1985, Susan Gollagher Toner wrote to me describing her last Christmas in Tin Cup. Here is her letter:

I especially remember our last Christmas in Tin Cup.

In preparation for this event we children had strung cranberries and popped corn in long strands to put on the large tree in the town hall. We had also cut out cardboard stars and covered them with silver colored paper. We had studied hard on the little skits and poems and learned Christmas carols for we always had a program with all the school children involved.

When the program had come to an end, the excitement grew as we knew Santa would soon arrive. I don't remember who played Santa in prior years, but the honors fell to Mr. Duran (Coyote Bill) in 1905. After the sleigh bells ceased ringing, Mr. Duran rushed into the hall with a "Ho, Ho, Ho." He at once started distributing the presents which had been brought in and piled under or tied on the tree by the parents before Christmas. Mr. Duran would cut the presents down, call out the name on it and then someone would pass them out.

There were cornucopias of candy, nuts and an orange for every child, mostly supplied by my Papa.

I'm not sure what each of us received, but this was the year Anne and I received skis. Katherine and Rose received theirs the year before. I remember I got a little red rocking chair which I prized highly. I also got a little doll cook stove (iron). I think we girls all got dolls (a must back then).

I know Papa brought the wheelbarrow that he delivered groceries in after the evening ended. It was full of presents as there were six of us then. Charles was born the next summer.

I especially remember our walk home as the moon was shining brightly, the stars seemed close enough to touch. The snow squeaked under our feet as it was so cold. It, too, glittered in the moonlight. A memorable event for an eight year old.

When we reached home the warmth of the wood burning stoves thawed us out.

I'm sure this was Christmas Eve for our stockings were hung along the mantle, but Mama and Papa said, "It's time for bed. No more excitement tonight."

P.S. There were other ornaments on the large Christmas tree besides the ones we made. These ornaments were kept from year to year with more being added. Of course there were many lighted candles to add to the beauty of it.

Dan Harrington remembers another Christmas Eve party in the town hall.

The children had finished their school program, the candles on the tree were glowing and Santa Claus had arrived. All went well with excited children receiving their gifts until Santa reached for a small gift tied to the tree. A nearby candle ignited his beard, the flames quickly spread to his red suit and the guests were frozen in fear.

"Three men reacted quicker than the others, grabbed the

flaming Santa and threw him through the foyer window into the soft snow," said Dan. The snow extinguished the flames, but Santa had to make an emergency trip back to the North Pole while someone else finished distributing the gifts. "I believe Pat Tomney was Santa that year," continued Dan.

Fortunately, Mr. Tomney was not seriously burned and his padded suit protected him when he was tossed through the window—he was ready to play his banjo for the dance that followed.

"Each year the large working mines closed from Christmas through New Year's and sent their cooks into Tin Cup to prepare feasts for both holidays," said Dan.

When the Christmas Eve party ended and the parents had taken their children home, the adults with no children stayed on and danced until the "wee hours," interrupted only by a huge smorgasboard served around midnight.

Dan continued, "Pat Tomney played his banjo, Harry Stiles played the accordion, and while Mrs. Lillian Churchill lived in Tin Cup, she played the piano. If shy Larry Englebright could be coaxed into it, he played his violin. Often a visitor in Tin Cup with musical talent played in the orchestra too.

"The New Year's Eve party was a big affair for the entire Tin Cup mining district," continued Dan. People came from miles around dressed in their finest clothes. The dancing started with a grand march to "break the ice" and to get everyone on the dance floor.

At midnight the dancing stopped, men set up large tables that lined both sides of the hall and the mine cooks, who tried to outdo each other, managed to outdo themselves each year. "The result was," according to Dan, "the tables were loaded with roast piglettes, turkey, beef, 'possum that the northerners would not touch but the southerners loved, vegetables from potatoes to turnips and desserts that wouldn't quit.

"When everyone had eaten, the dancing resumed and continued until dawn. No one had to hurry home to the children—they were all in the hall sound asleep on coats and lap robes in corners away from the dancers.

"Dances were held more frequently in the warm months when transportation was no problem. Cowboys tied their horses to the hitching rail east of the hall and wagons pulled up to the decking that skirted the south and east ends of the building. The ladies stepped from the wagons to the deck and on into the hall.

"There was always a lot of drinking by itinerate miners that resulted in fights, but before fights started in the hall, someone rushed the belligerent parties outside where they settled their differences."

Dan continued, "Each year on the 4th of July, someone set off a stick of dynamite at the crack of dawn; that really woke up the Tin Cup people! However, no one ever complained because that was the signal to start getting ready for the annual fish fry on Texas Creek in Taylor Park.

"The men left for the Park early in the morning on horseback with their fish poles. By the time the women and small children arrived about noon in wagons with all kinds of good food, the men had bonfires ready to fry their big catches of cutthroat and rainbow trout. The 4th of July was the big day of the summer months for the Tin Cup people."

It would seem the Tin Cup folks did not lack for entertainment and fun.

Ready for July 4 fish fry? Lowry Englebright, first man on left, Phil Korn, left of man on horse. *Courtesy Frances Taft.*

Tragic Events

An early settler related this story to the Morris family. This may have happened in 1864:

Before there was a Tin Cup Camp, Mr. and Mrs. Robert Whitelaw and infant made camp in what was to become Tin Cup. Mrs. Whitelaw was the first white woman among the many men prospecting for gold and silver.

Shortly after the Whitelaws had settled in, the mountain Utes became angry with the prospectors and, hoping to scare them out, they set the forest north of Tin Cup on fire. Mrs. Whitelaw had presence of mind to wet a handkerchief in a nearby spring and held it over her baby's face as they fled the fire and smoke. The Indians succeeded in scaring out the Whitelaws; nothing more was heard of them.

Dan Harrington said there was a forest fire north of Tin Cup many years ago that stopped just short of Tin Cup Lake (Lily Pond). Lodgepole pines have grown back and no doubt that ground was part of Forest Supervisor W.R. Kreutzer's reseeding program.

"Maude Woll, Frances and I saw a man shot," said Nettie. "There was a drunken brawl over a small amount of money that Mr. Lynch owed Mr. Connally for work Connally had done. The men were in Mrs. Ballenger's restaurant when the fight started. When they started cursing and threatening each other, they were ordered out of the building.

"The two men came half running and half stumbling out of the restaurant, across the boardwalk and onto the dirt road. As Mr. Connally turned away from Lynch reaching for his pocket,

Formerly Aunt Kate's, Ballenger's, and finally Hotel Rohm, 1909.
Courtesy Colorado Historical Society.

Lynch pulled his gun and fired. Connally dropped to the ground.

"Grandma Morris was with us and she hustled us home so no one would know we'd seen the shooting and force us to testify. We were about twelve and thirteen years old.

"Mr. Connally lived only a few days and Mr. Lynch was freed; however, his young wife said he was haunted by Connally and woke up screaming many nights."

A follow-up story about Mr. Lynch, courtesy Maude Woll Dobbins (*Gunnison—News Champion*, 1904):

John Lynch Killed in Accident

John Lynch, the well known Tin Cup mining man who has figured in so many murder trials at Gunnison, was killed Thursday evening about 5 o'clock. He was found dead in the road. Evidently he had been standing up in his buggy putting on an overcoat when the horse started, throwing him out. The wheels passed over his body and he was dead when discovered. Coroner N.J. Hyatt drove up that evening to the scene of the accident. Mr. Lynch leaves a wife and two children. He was interested in a great many mining enterprises in Taylor Park.

Koertenius (Charley) Latourette

Charley LaTourette has been written up as a vicious killer both in books and newspaper articles because in 1882 he killed the town marshal, Harry Rivers. The following may clear up some misinformation about the killing.

From a letter from Susan Gollagher Toner: "My great-uncle, Koertenius (Charley) LaTourette, was born in Fountain County, Indiana. When he was about 21, he enlisted in the 115th Indiana Regiment. At that time, most men enlisted for a year, so his next enlistment was in the 133rd regiment and then the 154th, where he was commissioned a first lieutenant in Company C. He served with this regiment until the end of the Civil War.

"About 1872 Charley went to Kansas where he married Emma Curtis. She was originally from Indiana also. Some time after this they moved to Leadville and were friends and neighbors of Augusta and Horace Tabor.

"The LaTourettes went to Tin Cup about 1879. Charley opened a saloon called The White House which made him rather unpopular with other businessmen in town who sold liquor.

"One evening when Charley was alone in his saloon, Mr. Rivers, the town marshall, came in and started berating my uncle and calling him vile names. Charley saw at once that Rivers was drunk and having no quarrel with the chap, he made Rivers leave and Charley decided to go home until Rivers sobered up; however, Rivers followed him and started shooting. As Charley neared his home a block away, it suddenly occurred to him that when his wife heard the gate squeak, she would unlock the door and open it as she always did when her husband came home. He also knew this would make her a perfect target for Rivers' bullets. At that instant, he drew his gun, whirled around, fired and Rivers dropped dead.

"A kangaroo court was held in Tin Cup and Charley was exonerated, but several of the townsmen insisted that the case be taken to Gunnison. Charley went to Gunnison voluntarily and again he was tried for the shooting and exonerated. The man who presided over the case was Judge Sprigg Shackleford. The court reporter was a Mr. Thomas whom Mother said was a cousin of Lowell Thomas.

"In the mid 1950s, my sister, Katherine, was visiting in Colorado and she hunted up Mr. Thomas. He said he remembered the case and that our version was correct. He told Katherine he would find his old notes and transcribe them for her; however, they both became ill and died shortly after and the notes were never transcribed.

"In the early 1900s, Aunt Emma and Uncle Koerty adopted a daughter, Victorine Sprankle. This adoption went through Judge Shackleford's court. Now, if Charley was such a lowdown, underworld character as some authors say he was, do you think a judge would have permitted him to have this child?"

Harry Rivers' brother, Charles, who lived in Denver at the time of the killing, went to Tin Cup for the funeral and when he returned to Denver, a reporter from the *Rocky Mountain News* interviewed him about the killing. In his version of the story, Harry Rivers was innocently walking down the boardwalk in front of Charley LaTourette's saloon when the latter stepped out of the building and shot and killed him. This version of the killing may be why Charley LaTourette became a cold-blooded killer to some writers.

Another great-niece, Rose Gollagher Stuart, writes: "I am very glad you sent me the article about Tin Cup's violent days. I had read some of the article and was incensed at the reference to our uncle, Mr. LaTourette, being a scoundrel. This is as far from the truth as it could possibly be, and I should like to refute this injustice to Mr. LaTourette. It was written to discredit him by someone who disliked him and to make their story exciting. There was violence I admit, but I prefer to remember the good part.

"This is the way my mother told it to me: Mr. Rivers, although he was sheriff, was not above violence himself. He entered my uncle's place of business and started an altercation with him about a former disagreement they had had. Mr. Rivers was drinking; he was so unreasonable that he was put out of the saloon. This angered him so much that he waited until Mr. LaTourette closed the saloon to go home. He followed Charley and shot twice at him. At the gate to his house, my uncle turned and seeing Rivers still coming with drawn gun, shot him in self-defense. Mr. LaTourette never went to trial. He stood preliminary hearing in Gunnison and was completely exonerated."

More information about Mr. LaTourette from Antoinette Morris Roy: "I wish I could go to Gunnison and go through all those old records of the trial of Charley LaTourette. According to the book Frances bought, he killed another man but he could have been entirely in the right. After all, the man may have threatened him, but they still paint him pretty black.

"Maybe he was for a while, but I remember him as always being friendly with us children and with my father and mother. I know I thought him an extremely nice man. I hope you can find something to paint him in a different light."

Carl A. Freeman

The following news item from the *Denver Post*, February 26, 1912, concerns one of the first businessmen in Tin Cup. Besides opening the first general merchandise/grocery store, Mr. Freeman owned the Bank of Tin Cup. Courtesy Maude Woll Dobbins:

Freeman, Once of Denver, Slain by Masked Bandits

Carl A. Freeman, formerly of Denver, one of the pioneers of the mining camp of Tin Cup, Colo., with extensive acquaintance in all mining districts of Colorado, was murdered at Mogollon, N.M., last week by

Tin Cup, Colo _____ 182 _____ No. 4283

Bank of Tin Cup.

C. A. Freeman and Co

Pay to the order of _____ $ _____

Dollars

TO THE PEOPLES NATIONAL BANK,
DENVER, COLORADO.

Courtesy Cora Nissen Luce.

masked bandits, who also killed his bookkeeper,
(William Clark) and escaped with $3,500 in cash, the
payroll for the Mogollon mines . . . .

Freeman was 56 years old, a native of Wisconsin. He
came to Colorado when a youth, and when the Tin Cup
boom was on, established the first general merchandise
store there. He was also interested in mines and became
very wealthy. His wife was Miss Lizette Tomlinson, once a
teacher in the schools of Denver, from one of the most
prominent families of Gilpin County. The family resided
in Denver, after leaving Tin Cup, until about ten years ago
. . . .

The "Alley" Girls

During the early boom days, 1880 to 1890, the red light district was located on the south end of Grande Avenue. As the boom slowed, many of the "night ladies" left for greener pastures, south Grande Avenue became respectable and the remaining "girls" moved to the alley buildings behind Washington Avenue, plying their trade in the nearby saloons, gambling houses and dance halls.

"Yes, we had dance hall girls in Tin Cup even when I was growing up," said Frances. "I remember seeing them from a distance from time to time. The girls didn't come outside very often in the daytime, but sometimes they'd come out in their shimmies with a bucket in hand and dip water from the ditch. The townspeople called them the "alley girls." They lived in buildings on the alley just north of the Woll-Niederhut store and behind some of the saloons and dance halls east of that store."

Nettie told this story about "Oh Be Joyful." "Papa told us a story about one of the girls when he was Justice of the Peace and the girls still lived in the red light district on south Grande Avenue in the late 1880s.

" 'Oh Be Joyful' was under contract to her madam, Deadwood Sal, for a certain length of time and Deadwood Sal held on to her 'girls' like many of the slave owners in the South held on to their slaves before the Civil War.

"A young rancher from the Gunnison area fell in love with 'Oh Be Joyful' and wanted to marry her, but Deadwood Sal held 'Joyful' to her contract. No amount of begging on the part of the young rancher and 'Joyful' would change the madam's

Alley buildings behind business places on Washington Avenue.
Courtesy Colorado Historical Society.

mind. The young man told two of his friends who lived in
Gunnison about his love for 'Joyful' and the hold the madam
had on her. After much discussion, the three young men
worked out a plan to rescue the girl.

"The rancher made a special trip to Tin Cup to tell 'Joyful'
about the plan and asked her to be ready to leave on a certain
night. He then went to see my father and asked him to marry
them on that certain night—if all went well. Of course, Papa
said 'Yes.'

"About a week later, on a moonless night, the rancher's two
friends arrived in Tin Cup and scouted Deadwood Sal's house
to be sure 'Joyful' was alone in her room. When they knew it

was safe to continue with their plan, they rented a horse-drawn wagon at the livery stable, loaded the town fire ladder on to the wagon and returned to Deadwood Sal's. With the ladder up to her window, 'Oh Be Joyful' carefully and silently climbed down with her few possessions in a small canvas case. The three young people ran to the waiting wagon on Grande Avenue and galloped south out of town.

"At the Slaughter House Road, they turned right, crossed West Willow Creek and slowly climbed the hill beyond the slaughter house for about a mile to reach the cabin where the bridegroom and my father were waiting.

"Papa married the rancher and 'Oh Be Joyful' in that little cabin in the hills and then he rode back home in the wagon while the young couple and their two friends left on horses the groom had brought from Gunnison. They rode into Union Park, followed Lottis Creek down Union Canyon to the Taylor Canyon road and on to the groom's ranch. Nothing was ever heard from Deadwood Sal regarding the matter.

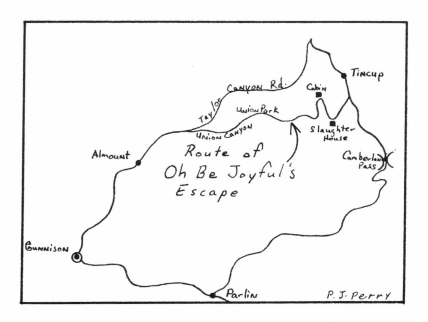

"Many years later, perhaps in the 1930s, my brother, Edward Morris, was visiting in Gunnison and met an elderly man in a restaurant. Edward told the man he had lived in Tin Cup and that his father was at one time a Justice of the Peace in Tin Cup. The conversation got around to 'Oh Be Joyful's' escape. When Edward finished the tale, the man quietly said, 'I was 'Oh Be Joyful's' husband until her death recently. She was a wonderful woman and together we raised a fine family and worked a good ranch. Young man, everything about 'Joyful's' escape from Deadwood Sal happened just as your father told you.' "

By 1899, life in Tin Cup had settled into day-to-day living, families were established and the women were "up in arms" about the few remaining alley girls; but before they were "run out of town" in 1900, Nettie told about meeting "Tin Can Laura."

"One day I was playing dolls with Elsie Bley at her home. Mrs. Bley was at the Tin Cup Merchandise store buying groceries when 'Tin Can Laura' came by Elsie's house to pick up the clothes Mrs. Bley had washed and ironed for her. They were beautiful clothes with lots of satin, ruffles on her skirts, and, oh the colors were so bright and cheery!

"To Elsie and me, Laura said, 'Be sure and mind your mothers. Your mothers know best. Mind everything your mothers tell you.'

"She did more for Elsie and me in that short speech than all the lectures on evil our mothers ever gave us because we knew what 'Laura' was. Shortly after I met her, 'Tin Can Laura' moved away. I heard later that she married and settled down on the east side of the Divide near Granite."

The Tin Cup School
and
The Tin Cup Jail

There is no longer any evidence of the one-room schoolhouse or the flagpole that stood out in front of the school or the hill upon which they stood. In September 1951 when we bought the Tin Cup Cabins from Mr. and Mrs. Merton Potter, the school building had already been torn down, but the foundation was there. The flagpole was still reaching to the sky, but in recent years it too has been removed and "schoolhouse hill" has been leveled. A modern duplex rental cabin stands on the spot today.

"In 1897 there were only two pupils in school on opening day," Nettie recalled. "To keep the teacher and to keep the school open, it was necessary to have three pupils so, at the age of five, I was enrolled in school. Later, Mr. and Mrs. Frank Reid and their four children, Boswell, Ben, Nettie and Dick, moved to Tin Cup and we had our quota of children; however, I was allowed to remain in school.

"The old schoolhouse was built of logs, covered with clapboards. There were two pupils to each old-fashioned desk with an opening underneath for storing our books, pencils and papers. Our wood stove was large and the big boys kept it well fed with two-foot logs. On mercilessly cold days in winter, our teacher gathered us round the stove to keep warm while we studied our lessons.

"On special holidays, we had many tableaus and charades. We also had to learn long poems and then recite them.

"Some of the teachers I remember well but others I've forgotten," continued Nettie. "Miss Lillian Sutton (Churchill) was an accomplished pianist and had a lovely singing voice. Miss Reynolds was a disciplinarian. You could hear a pin drop in her classroom, but just the same, we loved her. I remember her telling us, 'If you wish to chew gum, do it in the sanctity of your own room' "

Ione Miller (Jones), Oakland, California, who taught from

Lillian M. Sutton's school souvenir, 1903. *Courtesy Frances Taft.*

1904-05, said, "Teaching school in Tin Cup was a rewarding experience, I can assure you."

Frances Taft remembered, "Every winter the snow got at least three feet deep. Paths had to be kept cleared and packed down after each storm.

"We lived close enough to the school to walk home for lunch, but when fresh snow fell during the night, Mama packed our lunches and we'd roll to school in the newly fallen snow. It was difficult for short legs to walk in the snow when a foot or so fell through the night. As soon as we were big enough to ski, we skied to school.

"One winter a severe storm came up during school hours, and when it appeared the children would be unable to get home from school, some men came to the school with rope and made a rope trail from the school to the nearest home, which was our house.

In front of old schoolhouse, Arbor Day, April 20, 1906. Front row, left to right: Susan Gollagher, Ray Duncan, Mildred Whittenberger, Abbie Woll, Stanley Evilciser, Edna Lierle, Katherine Gollagher, Elmer Duncan, Ernest Duncan. Back row, left to right: Harold Whittenberger, Rose Gollagher, Merle Ballenger, Paul Bley, Frances Morris, Elsie Bley, Maude Woll, Rhoda Wilson. Teacher may have been Ione Miller. *Courtesy Rhoda Wilson Delucchi.*

"The teacher and the men guided us all along the rope in that howling blizzard to our house. The teacher and children stayed overnight with us while the men went on and notified the parents that all the children were safe. When that storm finally quit, we had five feet of snow on the level, but the men in town worked hard to keep the paths and roads passable and we went to school the next day.

"We children put on wonderful school plays in the first town hall that later became the Woll-Niederhut store (formerly the Masonic Building) and then in the new town hall, built in 1903," continued Frances. "The children would go around town to peoples' homes and borrow portiers—you know, heavy drapes—to use as curtains for our plays. Mama let us boil whole hams in a big boiler and we children made ham

Back row, left to right: first boy, unknown; Charlie Niederhut; Olive Niederhut; Antoinette Morris; Frances Morris; Maude Woll; Paul Bley; Ernest Duncan; Miss Bertha Williams (teacher). Front row: Elmer Duncan; Harold Whittenberger; Mildred Whittenberger; Ray Duncan. *Courtesy Frances Morris Taft.*

sandwiches and white and chocolate cakes to serve after the plays. Most of the town turned out for our school plays.

"If the current teacher could not furnish the music, Mama did; she played the piano, organ, violin, banjo, guitar and mandolin.

"One play I well remember was 'Tenting Tonight In The Old Campground.' Every pupil took part in the play and we must have enjoyed ourselves because we were a smashing success with our audience."

Frances also remembered an embarrassing incident. "Our school stove used long cord wood and it was cut and piled neatly beside the school ready for winter use. One fall, my sister, Nettie, George Norwood, some other children and I were playing on the wood pile when George pushed Nettie off.

Teacher, Mrs. Lillian
Sutton Churchill, back
row with scarf on
head. Girl to left of
teacher is Olive
Niederhut, niece of
Will Niederhuts.
Others cannot be
identified. *Courtesy
Frances Taft.*

She hurt her nose so badly, it was difficult to stop the bleeding.
When everything was finally under control and we were all
back in our seats, I went to the teacher's desk to ask a question
(I had taken my slate along), and on the way back to my seat, I
was still so mad at George for pushing Nettie off the wood pile,
I hit him over the head with my slate. The slate broke and he
ended up with the frame around his neck.

"My father was a school trustee, and when he was told what I
had done, he felt I had to be punished. I sat for one week in the
corner at school with a dunce cap on my head. I was 13 years
old!"

The following, courtesy Maude Woll Dobbins' unpublished
scrapbook:

Tin Cup School (1906)

This week the *News* received from Miss A.R. Reynolds, teacher, a report of the Tin Cup school for the past year, also a program rendered by the school on the 21st of this month. At the entertainment many of the parents and friends of the pupils were present and are pleased with the result of the year's work. The report and program are as follows:

Report of Tin Cup School

Number enrolled two months....................14
Number enrolled six months.....................7
Average attendance 7.6
Per cent of attendance 97.5
Per cent of punctuality........................ 98
Names of pupils neither absent nor tardy: Wilford Woll, Fannie Morris.
Names of pupils not tardy: Nettie Morris, Maude Woll, George Norwood.
Miss A.R. Reynolds, Teacher

Program of Entertainment:

The following recitations were delivered by the pupils:
Playing School .... Nettie Morris
Children and the War ....Fay Fogarty
I Can't; I Promised Mother .... Maude Woll
The Last Leaf.......................Fannie Morris
Sand ....Wilford Woll
Time Enough Yet .... George Norwood
The Naughty Little Comet............ Fannie Morris
Were I The Sun ....Fay Fogarty
Nellie's Dolls .... Maude Woll
I Got to Go to School ....Wilford Woll
The Ducks .... Tinella Fareman
The Patter of the Shingle .... George Norwood
The Ship On Fire .... Nettie Morris

(1906) Miss A.R. Reynolds returned Saturday from a three-months vacation spent at various points in the east to resume her duties as school teacher at this place. Miss Reynolds gave good satisfaction last year and the patrons are glad the school board secured her services for the ensuing year.

(1908) The pupils of the Tin Cup school rendered a very pleasing program on Friday the 21st in commemoration of the birth of Washington, under supervision of their most efficient teacher, Miss A.R. Reynolds. A number of the parents and friends were present and were most pleasantly entertained. A great majority of the pupils are almost kindergartners, yet the recitations rendered, and the manner of delivery would have done justice to those of much more mature age. This will make the fourth term that Miss Reynolds has taught the Tin Cup school, which fact alone speaks volumes as to her qualifications as a teacher.

Pupils taking part in the program were: Ernest Duncan, Harold Whittenberger, Victorine LaTourette, Ralph Duncan, Edward Morris, Mildred Whittenberger, Abbie Woll, Marie Harrington, Elmer Duncan, Sarah Tomney, James Harrington, Roy Duncan, Marguerite Tomney, and Theodore Duncan. Miss Reynolds' enrollment increased from seven pupils in 1906 to fourteen in 1908.

Rose Stuart and her sister, Susan Toner, who left Tin Cup in 1906, furnished me with a partial list of teachers: Misses Lillian M. Sutton, Bertha Williams, Ione Miller, A.R. Reynolds, Florence Goade, Alice Tice, Minnie Turner, — Mitchell, — Ketcham and Olive Woods. Susan said that except for Miss Sutton, who lived with her parents in Tin Cup, the teachers lived with various families in town.

My sister-in-law, Winifred Robistow, sent me the following clipping from the *Denver Post*, dated 8-10-76:

Ruby S. Stephan

Memorial services for Ruby S. Stephan, a retired school teacher and a certified graphoanalyst, were held Monday at Lakewood Presbyterian Church . . . . She first taught school in Tin Cup, Colorado in 1912 . . . . She is survived by a daughter, H. Mildred Hill, Rosemead, Calif., a son, Wilbur M. Stephan, Lakewood, Colo., and a sister, Mildred Moore, Evergreen, Colo.

I asked her son, Wilbur Stephan, if his mother ever told him about her year in Tin Cup. He said the wild stagecoach ride over Tin Cup Pass really impressed the then Ruby Simmons. She taught in Tin Cup one year and then went on to teach in the Pitkin school where her younger sister, Mildred, joined her.

Miss Anna Gill taught the last classes in 1916-17. She later married John Kirchover, engineer on the dredge (on Willow Creek, north of Tin Cup) and they moved to California.

The Tin Cup Jail

The Tin Cup jail was built in the 1890s, about twelve years after the first settlers moved into this 10,182-foot-high town.

Mr. and Mrs. Carl Wright of Oklahoma, who now own the jail, use it as a summer home. They have left two of the original three cells as they were and use them as bedrooms. The third cell has been converted into a kitchen and a window and back door were added in this room.

The combination living and diningroom was once the marshal's office, and this is where the only three exits, two windows and a door, to freedom were located. The Wrights have left the steel bars on the windows.

The original door to the jail was made of four 1½-inch thick knotty pine boards reinforced by more 1½-inch boards cut diagonally and secured with square nails braded on the outside. Each cell door was made the same. The ceiling of the jail is made of solid logs. There is no record of escapes from the Tin Cup jail!

The "bars" that separate the cells from the marshal's office may be the jail's most unique feature; half logs with the bark left on were securely installed three inches apart—no doubt to give the marshal a good view of his "guests."

Although the jail had only three cells, it was a busy place. Tin

East side of Tin Cup jail.
Courtesy Johanna Niederhut.

Log bars on cells, 1955.

Cup was a wide open mining town with shootings, murders and drunkenness. Twenty-six saloons and gambling houses operated night and day during the boom days and no itinerate preacher was encouraged to remain and establish a church.

Before the town hall was built, the jail was used as a voting precinct. "I remember going into the jail with Mama when she voted," said Nettie.

"Oh, Nettie, the women didn't get the vote until 1920 and we'd left Tin Cup by then," Frances said.

"But I think you'll find the women of Colorado could vote sooner," answered Nettie. "And I distinctly remember Mama voting in the jail and dropping her ballot into a box."

Nettie was right. The State of Colorado granted her women the right to vote in 1893. The women exercised that right for the first time in 1894 and promptly voted three women to the General Assembly! The year 1896 was a general election year, and Nettie would have been 4 years and 8 months of age in November. This is probably the election she remembered.

Tin Cup "Cemetary" sign, 1965.

Three graves on Jewish Knoll, 1952.

The Tin Cup Cemetery

Many people visit Tin Cup every year because of its unusual name, but many of the visitors are not aware that, in addition to its unusual name, Tin Cup has a unique cemetery—the Cemetery of Four Knolls. It might even be called a segregated cemetery. One knoll (the largest) is the Protestant Knoll with a section in the southwest corner set aside for Masons. Nearby there is a Catholic Knoll, a Jewish Knoll and a Boot Hill Knoll.

To reach the cemetery, go south on Grande Avenue to the sign marked "Tin Cup Cematary" (*sic*), turn east and go to the fork in the road. Turn left (the right fork takes you to the Gold Cup Mine). Drive a short distance to a slight rise in the ground and park your vehicle. This is the Jewish Knoll.

At one time there was a wagon road to each of the four knolls and possibly a road that came in from Tin Cup northwest of the cemetery; now all vehicles must be left near the Jewish Knoll. This knoll is much lower than the other three and is hard to recognize. When I first visited the cemetery in 1952, three wooden headboards on the Jewish Knoll had rotted at their bases but were still at the grave sites with no sign of other burials. The names and dates were legible and indicated that three infants of one family were buried there. The three headboards have since disappeared.

Boot Hill is on the highest, most centrally located hill in the cemetery—northeast of the Jewish Knoll. Deteriorating fences surround three poorly marked graves of men who died violently in Tin Cup during its heyday. There may be five graves on this knoll, and it is thought that one of the dance hall girls is buried on Boot Hill.

Boot Hill, 1965.

Kate Fisher, died 1902. *Author's photo, 1952. Courtesy Pueblo Chieftain.*

The Protestant Knoll is almost due north of Boot Hill—you can either jump a small creek or walk across a board that someone kindly places across the creek each year.

Kate Fisher, a Black lady, better known as "Aunt Kate," ran a popular boardinghouse in Tin Cup for many years. Aunt Kate's wooden grave marker has been moved to another area. Perhaps someone will find it and place it where the bearberries grow green on the Protestant Knoll no matter how dry the summer. The green bearberries mark Kate Fisher's grave.

Pioneer merchant Samual Gollagher was owner-operator of the Gollagher House, one of the largest general stores serving Tin Cup residents during the boom days. Mr. Gollagher's grave now has a contemporary grave marker added by two of his daughters, Rose and Susan, in the late 1950s. Mrs. Stuart told me about their trip to the cemetery with the marble gravestone:

"My sister, Susan, and I went to Tin Cup by truck accompanied by a young man from Grand Junction who placed the stone for us. We had to park the truck at the Jewish Knoll, unload the two-wheel dolly and gravestone and then walk around the beaver ponds to the plank bridge at the base of the Protestant Knoll. The 'bridge' would not hold up under the weight of the dolly and stone, besides being too narrow for the dolly. The young man waded through the icy water dragging

Samuel P. Gollagher.

the monument on the dolly, and then he pushed both up a steep incline about a quarter of a mile. Fortunately, some vacationers, seeing our predicament, helped us get the monument up onto the knoll."

Duncan Flats, three miles south of Tin Cup on the old wagon road over Cumberland Pass, was named after its founder, George Duncan, who is buried on the Protestant Knoll. A grandson of his made a special trip to Tin Cup with his bride in the mid 1950s to find the grave of his ancestor. They had no difficulty finding the grave which still had a legible marker. Duncan's grandson and his wife carefully replaced the stones outlining the grave and a few years later returned to place a marble marker near the wooden one which is now illegible.

The most recent burial in the Tin Cup Cemetery was in 1965. Lowry Englebright, who died two months short of his 100th birthday, had asked to be buried in Tin Cup. Because winter weather prevented an immediate burial, his remains were cremated and then buried after the spring thaw.

Services were held in the Tin Cup town hall and a simple marble headstone marks the final resting place of one of Tin

George E. Duncan.

Lowry Englebright.

LOWRY ENGLEBRIGHT
JUNE 17. 1865   APR. 14. 1965
PIONEER OF TINCUP

Cup's pioneer miners.

Frances Taft said her two baby sisters, Amaret and Burtona, are buried on the Protestant Knoll. "I remember there was an outcropping of marble not far from the cemetery and Mama and Papa fashioned two headstones from the marble to mark my sisters' graves. When Nettie and I came back for a visit in 1951, the marble headstones were gone."

Harry Rivers, who was killed in 1882 while serving as the Tin Cup marshal, is buried on one of the knolls.

The Catholic Knoll is east of Boot Hill. Just follow the well-worn path through the willow bushes. The graves on this knoll have not faired well through the years, with trees falling across graves, wooden fences rotting and falling to earth and wooden markers no longer readable. There are about 25 graves here and they extend to the east end of the knoll.

Not all of the people who died in Tin Cup could be buried in the local cemetery because as Dan Harrington, born in Tin Cup in 1910, said, "In the winter months burials were usually conducted in Buena Vista. The Tin Cup burial ground was frozen so deeply it would have required dynamite to open a grave."

While the toll road over Cottonwood pass was open, from

Grave on Catholic Knoll, 1968.

about 1880 to 1883, funerals traveling over the road to Buena Vista were allowed to go toll free—if they could prove they were transporting a body. The mourners paid the toll on the return trip.

For many years Frank Korn, an 1881 pioneer and uncle of Dan Harrington, and later Lowry Englebright carefully repainted in black the carved names and dates on the wooden grave markers. Even later, John Curtis, a former Tin Cup miner who spent three weeks each summer in Tin Cup, took over the board outlining for Mr. Englebright until the mid 1940s. When we first visited the cemetery in 1952, the wooden grave markers were easy to read. Today, many are gone, some are split and still others are too weatherbeaten to read.

Comings and Goings

Tin Cup had at least two newspapers in the 1880s with several newspaper name changes during that time. In later years, there was a Tin Cup news correspondent for one of the Gunnison papers, but the name of that writer remains a mystery.

The news items in this chapter are from the unpublished scrapbook of Maude Woll Dobbins. Where there is no date and no newspaper mentioned, a possible date and name of newspaper are in parenthesis. But first let's learn about the comings and goings of Jesse James in the Tin Cup area.

When I asked if Jesse James was ever in Tin Cup, Nettie quickly spoke up, "Indeed he was. Jesse, his brother, Frank, Charles and Bob Ford and one other member of their gang hid out in Captain Stiles' cabin at Dorchester (at the north end of Taylor Park).

"The Captain and his son, Harry, often visited our home and he told us about the James gang. It must have been about 1880 when they stopped at Stiles' cabin and asked for shelter. Captain Stiles said they were quiet, pleasant and caused no trouble at all. They helped out with chores around the cabin and did some prospecting. He said they stayed with him about three months."

When I mentioned to Dan Harrington that I had seen a dilapidated cabin on the Garden Basin road (about a mile west of Mirror Lake) where the James gang had hidden out, he replied, "It could very well have been. There were many rough characters who passed through Tin Cup in those early days." If the story I heard is true, perhaps the James gang traveled from

Dorchester, through Tin Cup and out over Tin Cup Pass on their way back to Missouri.

The first automobile in Tin Cup in 1905 created quite a stir.

Nettie recalls, "The word got out that a horseless carriage— an automobile—was coming to Tin Cup and the whole town was on the streets to greet it. The car was making a tour of various cities and towns and after its stop in Pitkin it was to come over Cumberland Pass to Tin Cup.

"The mayor of each town the car visited had to sign his name to a sheet of paper carried by a man traveling with the car. Sadie Hines' brother, Mike, was mayor of Tin Cup at that time, and I decided the best place to be to see this marvel was right at the mayor's house.

"The Hines lived on Grande Avenue just north of the East Willow bridge and Sadie and I took up vantage points on the road in front of her home and waited and waited for the car.

"We finally heard an unusual noise that grew louder and louder until there was the car turning from the Gold Hill road on to Grande Avenue. Cheering crowds lined the road as the car chugged down Grande Avenue and came to a dust-swirling stop where Mike Hines was waiting. Mike was the only one taken for a short drive down Grande Avenue in the car, but I touched it. It was splendid but to this day, I can't remember the make of the car. It was black and had a top, but that is all I remember."

Frances was at a different location when the car made its appearance.

"Yes, Nettie, you saw the car rolling into town under its own power that summer day, but I hiked up the old wagon road near Cumberland Pass to watch for the car. I can tell you why you, Sadie and the other Tin Cup people had to wait so long for the car. It did not come over the pass chugging—the altitude was too much for the car and it could not make it. In fact, it couldn't run in that altitude. A team of horses had to be found to pull it over the pass and down Gold Hill.

"When the car, horses and the men traveling with the car were about two miles south of Tin Cup where I was waiting, they stopped to unhitch the horses. While they were doing that and trying to start the car, I asked why they had horses pulling the car. That is when I learned the car could not run in high altitudes. They got the car started and went on down the rest of Gold Hill and on into Tin Cup.

"The team of horses followed discreetly behind the car and, during the ceremonies at Mike Hines' house, the horses turned up Washington Avenue and went up the Lake Catherine road. Later the car and its passengers headed for Lake Catherine and Alpine Pass. The horses had to pull the car over that pass too and on into St. Elmo"

The following, courtesy Maude Doll Dobbins: (Gunnison newspaper, 1907)

> Among those attending court at Gunnison last week were, W.W. Woll, Alex Parent, A.T. Harbert, Capt. Chas. Stiles, E.W. Wilding, Chas. LaTourette, A. Lajune, Dr. J.T. McGowan and Mrs. E.O. Churchill. (These people traveled via the Taylor River road which was a toll road!)
>
> C.T. Judy moved his family to Buena Vista the first of the week where the girls, Zoe and Ruth, will attend school.
>
> George Duncan and family returned from their old home in Indiana Wednesday where they have been during the past year, thinking a change of altitude would improve Mr. Duncan's health. He seems very much better. (Mr. Duncan died shortly after returning to Tin Cup.)
>
> (1908)
> Mrs. Annie Gollagher came in Saturday evening for a short visit and to settle up the estate of her husband, S. Gollagher, deceased.
>
> Pat Tomney was in from his ranch Thursday and reports a big hay crop.
>
> Frank Wareham returned Saturday from Salida, where he has been visiting his sister, and his son, Frank.
>
> Oscar Wolfe is wrestling with the grip.
>
> E.O. Churchill and wife have moved to St. Elmo. Ed is carrying the mail on that end.
>
> W.G. Niederhut left for Denver Friday. Harry Humphrey is handling the ribbons on the mail route during his absence.

E.O. Churchill came over from St. Elmo yesterday;
ever since landing has been brandishing his razor. Not
however, in search of blood but as a tonsorial artist.

French Baylor returned Monday. He, with his brother,
Frank, spent a part of last summer in our midst in the
belief that so glorious a climate must prove beneficial to
the latter's health. In this they were disappointed, and
during the winter returned to their home in West Virginia
where Frank died. French has opened up the Rohm Hotel.

Jas. Garden displayed rare ability as a broncho buster
on our streets Thursday. Anyone in need of "busting"
will do well to call upon or correspond with Mr. Garden.
Charges reasonable.

After all these years, the *Denver Post* has discovered that
there is a "little town in Gunnison county called Tin
Cup."

Larry Englebright, having tired of the gaiety of city life,
has hied himself to his country home, the Rat Trap, in
Taylor park.

Frank Vader, P.S. Roper and Wm. Duran (Coyote
Bill?) were in town Thursday bringing in the stock which
they had wintered.

Julius Hunsinger and Sim Irie are working the roads in
this corner of the county. Jule has been road overseer for
three years and gives excellent service in that line. The city
dads are also having the streets and alleys cleaned so we
will soon be doing turns in our autos. (!!)

From the *Douglass Tribune*, Douglass, Kansas, September 13,
1907. Courtesy, Maude Woll Dobbins:

> Miss Maude Woll of Tin Cup, Colorado, a niece of
> Mrs. James McCluggage, came in last Saturday to enter the
> Douglass High School.

There Were Church Services

"Ministers and Catholic priests came often to Tin Cup," said
Frances Taft. "They stayed at our house for days at a time and

church services of all denominations were held in the schoolhouse.

"I remember when Mrs. George Duncan was baptized," she continued. "A Congregational minister was in town that day and Mrs. Duncan's many friends helped make it a special occasion for her. She was dressed all in white and with her friends in a circle and Rothschild Mountain as a backdrop, she was baptized by total immersion in mountain-chilled West Willow Creek.

"When there was no minister in the town, our father performed weddings and conducted funeral services."

Susan Toner of Indianapolis, Indiana, remembers attending church services regularly in the school hall and, "A Mr. Hall, who lived in Abbeyville was in charge of our church services. He and his wife were very religious and conducted our Sunday school classes."

There Were Marriages

From the *Chaffee County Republican* (1904 or 1905), courtesy Maude Dobbins:

> Miss Carrie Murdie, daughter of Mr. and Mrs. Adam Murdie of Tin Cup, was married in Leadville on Easter Sunday to Joseph Jones. The bride has the distinction of being the first girl baby born in Tin Cup and the happy couple will go to housekeeping within 100 yards of where she was born.

Tin Cup Postmaster Weds Pretty School Teacher

Buena Vista, Colo., April 25. — Monday noon Miss Lillie Sutton, the handsome and accomplished school teacher at Tin Cup, was united in marriage to Edward O. Churchill of the same place in the parlors of the Princeton Hotel in this city . . .

There Were Divorces

The marriage of Lillian and Ed Churchill had an unhappy ending. The following is from a newspaper clipping, courtesy Frances Taft. The name of the newspaper is unknown and the date, but from other sources I have learned that this may have been news from 1914:

The caption under a picture of Mrs. Churchill reads: "Mrs. Lillian Churchill, who married the postmaster and a barber of Tincup, Colorado, and who taught school to support herself. The former postmaster was ordered to come up from Gunnison county and appear before Judge Rothgerber."

The following is from the text of the same article:

> Mrs. Lillian Churchill testified that she married Edward Churchill, a barber and postmaster at Tincup, Colo., in 1903, and that he gambled and ran the postoffice while she taught school to support herself; that he had not contributed to her support for more than two years. Judge Rothgerber ordered Churchill to come up from Gunnison county, where he lives, and tell his side of the story. The case was continued.

She was finally granted a divorce.

There Were Deaths

The following comes from a Gunnison newspaper, 1901:

> From her home in Tin Cup, Colo., after an illness of four weeks the spirit of the beloved wife of Alex Parent took its flight into the great unknown, Sunday morning, March 31, at 4 o'clock . . . The circumstances surrounding her death are peculiarly touching, having been the wife of Mr. Parent but four months . . . She was well known in both Pitkin and Gunnison as the wife of the late J.S. Wiley, and by whom she leaves a boy six years of age. The remains were laid to rest in the Masonic cemetery (Tin Cup) Tuesday afternoon, followed by her many sorrowing friends and neighbors . . .

Death of Samuel Gollagher

Prominent Tin Cup Merchant is Suddenly Stricken—
Well Known Over County

On last Monday evening our community was startled
and very much shocked at the sad news that Samuel
Gollagher, one of the pioneer residents of Gunnison
county, had died that evening at their residence in Tin
Cup, Colo. . . . Mr. Gollagher leaves to mourn him, a
mother, one sister and one brother in Ireland, and one
brother in Australia, a wife, five daughters and two sons.
The eldest, Kathryn, aged 11; Rose, 10; Susan, 8; Anne,
7; Gertrude, 5; Samuel, Jr., 4; and a baby a week old
(Charles), besides a host of friends, the entire community
and all who knew him. . . .

The interment was made in the Tin Cup cemetery,
services being held at the residence Tuesday, July 10th at
5:50 p.m., conducted by Harry Morris, who read the
Episcopal ceremony. The casket that contained the
remains was covered with flowers, the gifts of
innumerable friends. The concourse to the grave was the
largest ever witnessed in the town.

Death of Mrs. Frank Wareham
(1907)

The citizens of Gunnison were inexpressibly shocked
and grieved Monday to hear of the death of Mrs. Frank
Wareham, which occurred at Tin Cup, Sunday October
28 at 9 o'clock in the evening . . . Dolly E. Wareham was
born in El Paso County, Colorado, thirty years ago, her
parents moving to Gunnison county when she was five
years old, where she has since resided. On Nov. 7, 1897,
she was married to Mr. Frank Wareham . . . This death is
particularly sad, as there are five children left, all too
young to remember the dear mother, the oldest being
eight years, the youngest a babe of six weeks. A father,
mother, four sisters, three brothers and a husband are left
to mourn her death . . . .

Gold Cup Republic Tunnel. Man on left unknown; Will and Johanna Niederhut. *Courtesy Johanna Niederhut.*

Mining

Tin Cup never produced any Horace Tabors, but there were rich gold and silver deposits ready and waiting for those who were willing to work or had strong financial backing.

A Denverite, C. Hord, heard about the placer gold discoveries of the 1860s and 1870s and grubstaked a Captain Hall, specifying to Hall that he wanted no placer claims. Hord wanted the real thing—the mother lode.

Hall made his way to Tin Cup in 1878, surveyed the three streams that junction just west of town and headed up Middle Willow Creek. Three miles southeast of town he found what he was looking for; it became the Gold Cup Mine. After staking their claim, Hall returned to Denver with ore samples which Hord had evaluated. It was a rich find from the grass roots down.

The two men sold their property to the Bald Mountain Mining Co. for under $400,000. The Gold Cup became the heaviest producer of gold ore in the Tin Cup district followed closely by the Little Gold Cup, The Silver Cup and the Addie, all owned by the same company. The "Jimmie Mack" mine, owned by the E.C. Stoddard Co., ran a close second, shipping as many as 100 sacks of high-grade ore each day.

As a small child in the 1890s, Frances Taft remembered advance men arriving in town warning people off the streets and roads when a jack (burro) train loaded with ore was about to go through Tin Cup on the way to the smelter. The ore was heavily guarded with armed men a few feet apart along the "train."

The following mining news is from the unpublished

Star Mine, Italian Mountain, Harry Morris sitting on ground. *Courtesy Frances Taft.*

scrapbook of Maude Woll Dobbins, *Gunnison-News Champion*, 1901:

The Italian Mountain Sale

Last Saturday there was consummated in this city one of the largest mining deals, both in amount of consideration and prospective value to the town and county, which has taken place in Gunnison county for years. For several weeks it has been known that such a deal was in progress, but not until Saturday night were the papers signed and the money paid. The property sold was the Star Mine on Italian Mountain, and a number of adjoining claims. The Star was owned by Charles Hubbard, William Haynes, John McManus and Gus

Olson, and sold for $50,000. The other properties sold were: The Independent, owned by Gus Youngberger, Gus Olson and Peter Swanson, for $3,000; the Springfield, owned by Messrs. Haynes, Hubbard, McManus, Wm. Roof and W.W. Woll, for $2,000; the Italian, owned by Chas. Woll, for $500, and the Crown Points, 1 and 2, owned by Messrs. Haynes and McManus, for $21,000. Fifteen thousand dollars was distributed among these men Saturday night as a partial payment on their properties, the bank having been held open until a late hour for that purpose while the transfer papers were being made out and signed. The balance of the purchase money will be paid on August 1, 1901.

The purchaser of the property is Henry B. Gillespie of Denver who is said to be at the head of a strong company. He has already ordered a saw mill and hoisting machinery and next spring will erect a mill to treat the ore. Work will be pushed vigorously and in another year the Star promises to be among the great mines of the state.

Part of Gold Cup Mine, 1954.

The Gold Cup Mine is being operated from the ninth to the eighth level. In the eighth level a winze is showing a fine body of ore that carried high values in silver. The Gold Cup has been a heavy shipper.

The Bonnie Belle lode on Gold Hill is also in some fair ore, which was recently opened. Two feet of the vein runs $18 in gold and silver per ton.

All was not good news (1908):

E. Norliff, who has been teaming at the Blistered Horn for a year is taking a vacation on account of the soft snow roads.

Phil Korn has worked upon his Rothschild property a portion of the winter and the results are very gratifying.

Dick Reid has been prospecting on the same hill and reports he has struck "ile."

The management of the Blistered Horn are having great difficulty with bad air. They have installed a fan but lack power to keep it running. Louis Gendron who runs the hoister at the back of the tunnel, together with several others have been overcome. We hope the matter will soon be remedied.

By 1918 all the working mines had shut down.

Tin Cup Up To Date

By 1927 there was little activity, there were no stores and few people in Tin Cup. Hugh Corrigan Sr. and his family and Ralph Barron and his family discovered the town in the late 1920s and established summer residences. There was a slow but steady influx of tourists in the 1930s; some became enchanted with this isolated hamlet, bought property, repaired and upgraded the wooden homes and preserved a "ghost town."

When my husband, Maurice, and I bought the Tin Cup Cabins in 1951, there were about 150 summer residents, and except for a few, the old cabins were in excellent condition. We had 12 cabins to rent, Maurice added a room to the front of our living quarters that became the Tin Cup Store, and we had a hand-operated gas pump—Tin Cup's business district.

Three months later Maurice died, but with the help of my two sons, Bill, 10, and Pete, 6, my late mother, Helen Limoges, and my sister-in-law, Winifred Robistow, we kept the business going each year from the first day of fishing in late May to November 1 until 1959, when we sold the business.

Early in 1952 I tuned in to Denver radio station KTLN and caught "Pete Smythe's General Store, broadcast by simulated remote control from Tin Cup, Colorado." This happened on a day when the mayor of Tin Cup, Pete Smythe, was telling a listener that, except in his imagination, Tin Cup, Colorado, did not exist.

My hackles went straight up and I headed for pen and paper. In response to my letter telling Pete there was a real Tin Cup, Colorado, maps showed Tin Cup, and the fact that I owned the real Tin Cup Store, Pete Smythe invited Bill, Pete and me to

Tin Cup, 1927. Courtesy Robert Walker, Little Art Studio, Gunnison.

his store. Not only did we have the pleasure of meeting Pete and his announcer, Conrad Schader, we met Elmy Elrod, producer-director of the program, Moat Watkins and Alice Kefauver. We sat around the pot-bellied stove and listened while Pete played his piano, the African Queen, and visited with Homer Snerdley when he stopped by the store. Bill and Pete Perry wanted to meet Coach Rocky Head, but he was putting his unwinning football team through their final twelve-hour practice down in Doc Robin's pasture—the next day they were to meet with their arch rivals, Cement Creek High, and Coach Head allowed no "possible spies" for CCH near the pasture.

By 1953, "Pete Smythe's General Store" had moved to KOA radio and KOA-TV, where the program was eventually "simulated remote controlled" from East Tin Cup, Colorado. Many of his faithful listeners will remember Pete's opening song, "I put the key in the door, open up the store and now we're ready for business . . ." and his slogan, "Tin Cup, the slowest growing town in the nation and we aim to keep it that way" should bring back memories.

The real Tin Cup was slow growing through the 1950s, but thanks to Pete Smythe, it was becoming famous. Daily, people visiting our store asked, "Has Pete Smythe ever been here?" By May 22, 1954, we could say "Yes." On that date, Pete, the late Ken White, radio editor for the *Denver Post*, and several others from KOA visited us in Tin Cup. Not only did Pete Smythe visit Tin Cup, he has been a Tin Cup property owner for about 30 years.

Pete Smythe at Tin Cup, 1954.

Pete Smythe at Tin Cup town hall, 1954.

Today, a few more cabins are being built, many are being upgraded and electricity has come to Tin Cup. A number of the summer residents have private wells and "all the comforts" of home. There are no telephones, no parking meters and no smog in Tin Cup. The business district now consists of two restaurants, one store and one electrically operated gas pump (regular only).

The rental cabins we owned and the six rental cabins the late Mr. and Mrs. Chester Weiss owned are now all privately owned. There is one completely modern duplex available to rent, a small trailer and the "wash house" has been converted to a rental. Cabins are available at Holt's Ranch and at Sherman Cranor's at Taylor Reservoir, six and eight miles north of Tin Cup.

We were in Tin Cup for nine years and I remember: the time the family of four (father, mother and two young children) drove off the Cumberland Pass ledge road midway down the

Tin Cup Store, 1985—the Forest Service headquarters in 1905.

Frenchy's Cafe, 1985.

Tin Cup side. Every available adult in town, including tourists, rushed south to Cumberland and helped bring the injured father up the mountain side to a waiting station wagon. A tourist took him to the Gunnison Hospital where he recovered from his injuries. Fortunately, the mother and two children were not injured.

I remember when little 3-year-old Kathy (last name escapes me) of Pueblo wandered away from her family camp above Taylor Reservoir late one afternoon and was lost all night; it was the first warm night of the summer season. Word reached our store at 5:30 p.m. that Kathy was lost, and by 6:00 p.m. Bill and others from Tin Cup were on their way north to join in the search.

The next day the president of Western State College, Gunnison, was holding his annual picnic. Early in the morning, he asked the students and faculty if they'd be willing to take their food to Taylor park and help in the search for Kathy. Everyone was in agreement. One member of that group found the little girl at 11:00 that morning sitting by a tree on the hillside, talking to herself.

I remember when a man was nearly killed in our kitchen— shades of Tin Cup gone by?

Guy Cox, president of the Gunnison Chamber of Commerce, Wally Foster, editor of the *Gunnison News Champion*, and Ray Grabus, Denver, were visiting at our kitchen table. A tall, heavy man renting the cabin next door came into the store demanding to know who owned the car blocking his parking space. I said I would ask Ray to move the car right away. He did, but was too slow to suit the renter.

A few minutes later, Bill motioned to me to come into the store. Before I could walk through the living room to the store, the renter came around the counter headed for the kitchen, drunk, swearing mad and with a rifle; he was "going to kill that . . ."

I screamed to Bill and Pete to get under their bed and headed for the kitchen, where everyone was on their feet by this time. The rifle was inches from Ray's stomach and he was rapidly explaining that the car belonged to a crippled friend and had hand controls that he was not used to. That didn't matter, the

Mother Lode Cafe, 1985.

Inside Mother Lode Cafe

man was still going to kill Ray.

I don't know who did it, Cox or Foster, but one of them shoved the man and the other grabbed the rifle. The gouge in the back door caused by the rifle butt was still there when we left in 1959. The next morning I asked the "guest" never to return to our cabins. He had been a regular renter and had never caused trouble—once was enough.

One day a young Texas boy, visiting the Carlton Woodwards for the summer, was trapped on the mountain just east of Tin Cup and calling "Help . . . help!" We all heard him; people searched and researched every nearby hill but couldn't find him—his calls for help echoed off Rothschild Mountain and couldn't be pinpointed. An hour passed and he was still trapped. Nearly two hours later, after exhausting all possibilities, Hugh Corrigan III with other men came back to Grande Avenue, where the boy's calls for help were the clearest, and listened again. The men took off on a trail north of the Corrigan home. They had searched this trail before but had not gone quite far enough. They found the boy trapped under a fallen tree about a quarter of a mile further down the trail. His injuries were minor.

Tin Cup and its people haven't changed much from the very earliest days. In time of need, everyone still pitches in and helps, and I believe Hugh Corrigan III was in on every rescue mission in the 1950s and no doubt he still is today.

I remember the day some tourists left a smoldering picnic fire near a big log on the point near West Willow Creek at the

Grande Avenue, looking north, 1985.

foot of Rothschild. I had first seen them from our kitchen window around noon. About two hours later, they had left and the log was burning. I hollered to Bill, Pete and Joe Crowley, a classmate of Bill's spending the summer with us, to grab buckets, shovels and gunnysacks and toss them into the Jeep— we were going to a fire.

The rotted log made great fuel for the fire, and the forest was close but the four of us hauled water, shoveled dirt and had the fire completely out in about 45 minutes. The forest ranger stopped by the store about a week later, and I told him what we had done. He went to look over the burned area and much to our surprise, in about a month we each received a United States Government check for $20. I didn't know you got paid for protecting "your home" from fire.

I also remember the cloudless, perfect summer day when Peter and I were returning from Sherman Cranor's store. We were on the flats north of Hillerton when I pointed out to Pete a tiny cloud curling its way above Fitzpatrick Peak, south of Cumberland Pass. Suddenly I knew, "Peter, that is no cloud, that is smoke." I stepped harder on the gas pedal and just as we reached our store, a car was approaching from Cumberland Pass. The driver said, "Yes, there is a forest fire out of control north of Pitkin."

Bill hitched a ride south and worked that fire for two days. When he returned, he was dirty, exhausted and never wanted to work a forest fire again. I asked why. He answered, "Mom, it is the saddest thing in the world to see terrified animals, big and small, running ahead of a fire."

I remember the fun times too—the "come as you are breakfasts," the fish fries at Mirror Lake, the Saturday night dances in the town hall, the delicious dinners at the homes of friends, the 25-Jeep caravan. Peter remembers having to pump gas for those Jeeps; remember, this was a hand-operated gas pump—the gasoline always had to be hand pumped to the top of the bowl before dispensing gasoline to the next Jeep. His arm was pretty sore when the last Jeep was filled.

Another time the Range Riders from Colorado Springs camped for three days in a tree-edged meadow south of town. The late Lillian and Phil Moore, formerly of Colorado Springs, and I sat on the hillside watching the horse races on Grande Avenue. We even did a little betting.

There were many fun times during those nine years, but perhaps what I treasure most are the lasting friendships we made. Tin Cup is changing and growing a little, but it is also being preserved for generations to enjoy. Some things won't change—the endless ranges of mountains that ring the town and the intense blue of the sky.

Each time I visit Tin Cup, walk its streets or tread the boards of the town hall, I shall listen for those little girls of so long ago, Susan and Rose, and the late Maude, Frances and Nettie somewhere in the distance laughing and skipping along. They loved Tin Cup as I do and I hope you will.

Printed and Bound by:

Inter-Collegiate Press, Inc.
Shawnee Mission, Kansas 66201

Typesetting and Design by:

Shadow Canyon Graphics
Evergreen, Colorado